HEY THERE, COSTCO MEMBERS!
A SPECIAL HELLO TO YOU FROM ROCCO DISPIRITO

Before you cook from this book, I want to make one thing crystal clear: THIS IS NOT A DIET BOOK! I will not ask you to follow a strict regime of planned meals. There is no cleanse. No list of "ten foods you must buy today!"

THIS BOOK, just as with my very first, *Flavor,* is a classic cookbook in every sense of the word. It contains almost 250 recipes and more than 250 photos to make things easy. These recipes were designed for deliciousness and pleasure. Cooking them will be fun and easy. Eating and serving them will be sheer joy. The fact that they are also healthy—nutrient dense, free of substances such as gluten, dairy, and refined sugar—is neither a coincidence nor an obstacle to your enjoyment.

I have been advocating for a healthy lifestyle since I was confronted by my trusted family doctor about my own declining health in 2005. After years of hearing him say, "Don't worry, you are young and healthy," there finally came a day when he warned me of my imminent demise due to an excessive lifestyle. It was, to say the least, sobering. He told me I had the metabolic age of a sixty-eight-year-old man. I was thirty-eight at the time. He prescribed three medications and ran through the list of side effects, which were appalling. I asked naïvely, "Do I have other options?" Turns out, I still had a lot of other options. Thankfully, I was still healthy enough to make changes to my lifestyle that would improve my health. With this special edition, I hope to share the results with you.

I am excited to partner with Costco to offer this special edition of my cookbook because our missions are aligned: we both believe that high-quality, healthy, delicious, and affordable food should be available to everyone. That's why the recipes in this book are specifically designed to be both delicious and doable—plus really good for your health.

We are also pleased to offer Costco customers a special invitation to try $50 worth of *Rocco's Healthy + Delicious* products. Visit RoccoDiSpirito.com/costco50 for $50 off your first Rocco DiSpirito product. I hope you enjoy them as much as I do, and that they help you become confident in your kitchen every night, long into the future.

Rocco DiSpirito & the team

ALSO BY ROCCO DISPIRITO

ROCCO'S HEALTHY+ DELICIOUS

MORE THAN 200 (MOSTLY) PLANT-BASED RECIPES FOR EVERYDAY LIFE

ROCCO DISPIRITO

HARPER WAVE

An Imprint of HarperCollinsPublishers

This book contains advice and information relating to health care. It should be used to supplement rather than replace the advice of your doctor or another trained health professional. If you know or suspect you have a health problem, it is recommended that you seek your physician's advice before embarking on any medical program or treatment. All efforts have been made to assure the accuracy of the information contained in this book as of the date of publication. This publisher and the author disclaim liability for any medical outcomes that may occur as a result of applying the methods suggested in this book.

First Edition

Photography by Joanthan Punisnk
All images copyright by Flavorworks

Library of Congress Cataloging-in-Publication Data has been applied for.

ISBN 978-0-06237812-5

17 18 19 20 21 LSC 10 9 8 7 6 5 4 3 2 1

Contents

Introduction

I've dedicated my life to proving that healthy and delicious are not mutually exclusive concepts. Contrary to popular belief, you don't have to sacrifice flavor to eat well. You can be healthy, lose weight, and still enjoy amazing food all day long.

THE PROOF is in the cookbook you're thumbing through right now. There are more than two hundred recipes here—including plenty of satisfying meals and decadent desserts. And each one is made with healthy, great-tasting ingredients that will soon become your go-to pantry staples.

When I started working on this book, I knew one thing for certain: I didn't want to write a traditional "diet" book, with boring diet theory, philosophy, charts, and complicated shopping lists. And from the conversations I've had with you, my readers, I know that's not what you want either. Over and over people tell me that what they really want from me is more recipes to help them live a healthy life. Well, friends, here they are!

All of the recipes in this book are inspired by the dishes I make every day for my food delivery service customers. I prepare delicious meals that are delivered right to their doors, wherever they are—at work, at home, or on vacation, anywhere in the country. All of the meals I make are sourced from fresh, local, organic ingredients that are nutrient dense, gluten-free, dairy-free, and sugar-free. With these recipes at your fingertips, you too can live like you have a private chef and change your health and well-being for the better.

My personal journey to eating healthier began with a scare. I was a restaurant chef for many years, trained to prepare food with lots of butter or other fat, pour delectable sauces over it, and sugar it up, all with no regard to calories, nutrients, or anything else health-related. It didn't have to be good for you, it just had to taste good. And to make sure I was serving the very best food to my customers, I routinely sampled my creations. Over the years, that sampling added up, and my weight soared.

By 2008, my doctor told me that my cholesterol and blood pressure were creeping upward. He gave me two options: start taking medication or improve my diet and exercise. I remember thinking, Why don't I do the harder, smarter thing? I decided to learn how to make healthier versions of my favorite foods—and commit to a real exercise routine. A year later, I was thirty pounds lighter and much healthier. That's when I knew I was onto something, and a new, different sort of passion for cooking took hold.

At the time, there wasn't another chef within spitting distance (save for a few very brave souls—Michel Nischan and Matthew Kenney come to mind) who embraced a healthier lifestyle, much less was willing to transform their signature cuisine into healthier cuisine. The movement for "healthy and delicious" was small, sporadic, and weak. Those of us who were interested in nutrition were considered alternative types who craved wheatgrass juice and carried water bottles. My peers thought I'd lost my mind. No one could have imagined a day when made-to-order salad joints and juice shops could be found in any city.

As I began this journey, I developed a working set of parameters: re-create comfort food, shave off fat and carbs, and make sure the result was under 350 calories per serving—without making the dishes taste like cardboard. I was okay with using conventional foods, artificial sweeteners, "low-fat" sauces, and "sugar-free" stuff made with sucralose. As long as I got the flavor right and the calories under 350, I considered it a job well done. It was a huge undertaking and very ambitious for me at the time. The result was a book called *Now Eat This!*, and it was an instant success.

But in the years since then, I've refined my definition of healthy eating. I've cut out refined sugars and processed foods. I don't use artificial flavorings or sweeteners. I avoid gluten, dairy, and sugar. And I always try to source the best-quality ingredients—local and organic—whenever possible. These foods are higher in nutrients, free of pesticides and other toxic chemicals, and simply taste better. What's more, they're great for weight loss because their calories are used efficiently by the body, making them less likely to be stored as fat.

Today, consumers are more educated than ever before about the quality of their food. Most of you have heard about the dangers of high-fructose corn syrup and genetically modified organisms (GMOs). You know to read food labels. You know to avoid added sugars and preservatives. You know to run in the opposite direction from any and all trans fats.

A whole new language has evolved when it comes to food and wellness. Locavore, vegan, pescatarian, Paleo, ketogenic—the list goes on and on. So much is happening that requires a person like me to be vigilant, relentless, and dynamic. I'm always on the prowl for new ingredients, new techniques, new and better information to replace or refresh what I'm doing in the kitchen. The chef I was ten or twelve years ago is not the chef I am today. I am in perpetual metamorphosis!

Which brings us up to the "now." The food in this book is—just as it says on the jacket—mostly plant-based (and completely delicious). What does that mean? It means eating as close to the source as possible. I don't like to label the way I eat; instead, I just strive to cook with the healthiest ingredients I can find and let the results speak for themselves. That's why you won't find a lot of diet dogma in this book, just a few simple guidelines that will help you make better choices at the grocery store (more on that in Chapter 1). For now, I just want you to commit to one thing: eating real food that is healthy and delicious.

The recipes in this book are organized into two parts. In Part II, you'll find conventional categories like morning, mains, sides, salads, desserts, and snacks. I wanted to make the transition into eating more whole foods as easy as possible, and most people are used to thinking about their meals within a traditional framework. But I also wanted to provide a way for you to think about and plan your meals based on ingredients: healthy and delicious (mostly) plant-based meals, and many of the recipes require little to no cooking time. From simple dishes like my Avocado Furikake (page 284) and Eggplant Walnut Dip (page 255) to grab-and-go snacks like my Cocoa-Nutty Trail Mix (page 274) and Protein Almond Butter Balls (page 73), many of these recipes come together in as little as five to ten minutes and offer innovative ways to incorporate more nutritious foods into your day.

You don't have to follow a set of rigid dietary rules or learn a whole new vocabulary to start making wholesome, plant-based meals. The recipes in this book are foolproof and don't require any fancy equipment (my grandmother made some amazing food with nothing but a broken paring knife and a beat-up frying pan). So start eating more wholesome, plant-based foods. I just want you to get in your kitchen, cook, and have fun.

When you start cooking more, you'll find that your whole life changes for the better. It's no exaggeration. You will be a better partner and parent (I don't know of a better way to express love than to cook for someone), you'll save money by not eating out as much, you'll feel happier and more energetic, and you'll prevent a bunch of scary diseases in the process. The sooner you get behind the stove, the sooner you can start eating wonderful food that will make you and your family healthy and happy. If this chef can get healthy, anyone can!

Recipe Index

PART I

CHAPTER 1

Have You Heard? Healthy and Delicious Are Not Mutually Exclusive Anymore

Chefs don't usually reveal their secrets, but I'm going to bare all. It's one thing to state that healthy and delicious are not mutually exclusive, but another to actually explain how to make nutritious food taste phenomenal. You've got to know some tricks of the trade, and I'm sharing them here.

START WITH "REAL FOOD"

Real food is what our grandparents simply called *food*. Real food includes plants that come from the ground and fresh provisions that can be purchased at the local butcher or bakery. Real food is broccoli, almonds, fresh fish, and fresh fruit—the kinds of food that don't need packages, or even labels. The problem is, we've lost touch with the concept of "real food." We've become accustomed to buying our groceries at the same place we get our tires changed.

Real food is what the simplest, and often most satisfying, meals are made from. Have you ever noticed how some people can just toss together a few fresh vegetables and herbs with a little meat, chicken, or seafood and turn out a delicious meal? That is the sign of a true cook: the ability to create something dazzling in its simplicity. Salmon glazed with orange marmalade served with grilled asparagus fits my definition of a real, simple meal. It is gutsy, robust, and quick. It makes a great meal for two on a weeknight and is just as appropriate for a special dinner.

BUT ARE THERE ENOUGH REAL FOOD CHOICES IN THE MARKETPLACE?

Yes, if you ask for them—and look for them.

I often tell the story about how I walked into a Whole Foods once and asked the produce manager where the apples came from. His response was "not sure, overseas somewhere." His answer puzzled me because we were in New York City. It was September, and local apples were peaking. I asked him if he could try to find local apples since they were so easy to acquire and so delicious. I knew this because I had just visited the Union Square Greenmarket, and it was flooded with new-crop apples, pears, and other orchard fruit. I bought them by the wooden crate for my fresh food delivery clients. I also ate them voraciously. His response was, "Yes, I'll try."

A week later, I walked into the same store, and you'll never guess what I encountered. Not one, not two, but more than a dozen varieties of local apples with a little sign in each bin that indicated their provenance. The signs were clearly labeled with the variety of each apple, the state and farm of origin, and sometimes even the farmer's name and other esoteric bits of information. It was like a Match.com profile for apples!

The manager hadn't known I was a chef or worked in the food industry, so I'm convinced this had been an open topic for Whole Foods and that my refusal to buy an apple that traveled five thousand miles to get to me was enough ammunition for him to go to his people and insist that the store stock more local produce than non-local foods.

The choices available to us are partly our responsibility and partly out of our hands. Today there seems to be a "conscious uncoupling" between us and our food suppliers. It's now possible for a small food producer to sell direct to retail, without the filtered system of wholesalers, food brokers (yes, that's a real thing), distributors, and big food manufacturers. This is a quantum leap for the food industry and for thoughtful food manufacturers both large and small. I am one of those small food manufacturers who benefits from the new economy of food. I get to choose what I sell and in what form.

Even so, I'm often met with resistance when negotiating for real food ingredients. I've heard every excuse in the book from suppliers: "Organic is too expensive . . . it's hard to procure . . . people don't believe it's real . . . the certificate is too hard to get . . ." and many more. But I persist because I'm an advocate and an activist for local, organic, and whole foods—in other words, *real food*. And you can do the same. It will help break open the barn doors and give every one of us more options.

Prepared well, real food will always be more palatable and tasty than highly processed food. Plus, it's a better source of nutrients. It's food without the bells and whistles—just the flavor. Here are a few strategies to make it easy to incorporate more whole foods into your life:

Shop at Farmers' Markets

My grandmother grew her own food, and we ate what she grew, so I've been in tune with seasons from an early age. Before supermarkets were stocked with our favorite foods year-round thanks to refrigeration and shipping, that's the way everyone lived.

Today the rise in popularity of farmers' markets makes it possible for everyone to eat seasonally again. Your local farmers' market is brimming with produce that is fresh, in season, and grown locally. Buying "in-season" fruits and vegetables helps ensure that they are ripe and bursting with flavor and nutrients.

Keep a Supply of Flavor Staples

There are five things you'll always find in my kitchen, and I use them all the time to make healthy food taste delicious:

AVOCADO. It's one of my favorite snacks: I halve it and season it with soy sauce, sesame seeds, and lemon juice. I have an entire section in this book devoted to the glorious avocado.

HOT SAUCE. I put hot sauce on just about everything: eggs, pasta, pizza, steak, and fish.

ONIONS. This is one of the most versatile vegetable you can have on hand. It's great for adding flavor to your sautéed dishes, of course, and it can also be added to soups, sauces, and vinaigrettes. Just microwave a peeled onion for ten minutes, then blend it into anything you like.

FRESH HERBS. There's no dish—other than chocolate mousse—that can't be improved by the addition of fresh herbs. Remember, it's always best to add them at the end of cooking so they retain their flavor.

BLACK PEPPERCORNS. Yes, good old black pepper, from a pepper mill. I'm not being silly or calling out a mundane ingredient. Pepper in a mill makes a *big* difference. For a small investment, you will reap a huge reward in the flavor of your food.

Get Creative in the Kitchen

Chefs love experimenting and trying new combinations of food and flavors, overlapping them until a different taste emerges, and I'm no exception. I have a passion for deconstructing classic "restaurant" dishes and making healthier versions of them. One of the first dishes I toyed with was lobster bisque. Turns out that it actually tastes better when it's made with lower fat liquids than when it's made with cream!

One of my secrets for making dishes that are both healthy and delicious is to create "tension" in the food—by balancing sweet, salty, bitter, and sour flavors until the combinations captivate the taste buds. So I pair ingredients like miso with orange, and cherry preserves with Dijon mustard. That tension is what drives a lot of ethnic cooking, particularly in Southeast Asian and Indian cuisine. This is my own take on that approach to food.

To re-create the mouthfeel, flavor, texture, look, and aromas of foods you've been eating (in their unhealthy versions) your entire life, you've got to use a little creativity. The recipes here are a good place to start—they offer a gateway to new ingredients and food combinations. Once you're comfortable with them, I encourage you to improvise on your own!

As you start trying my recipes, I'll spill more of my secrets . . . and I guarantee you'll cook up some of the healthiest, most incredible meals ever and have fun doing it. You'll find plenty more of my chef secrets in the pages to come. I'm just getting started! Healthy food is delicious food—and the proof is in these recipes. But before we get cooking, let's talk for a minute about what exactly "plant-based" means. . . .

CHAPTER 2

WTF Is (Mostly) Plant-Based?

Friends, family members, and clients often ask me why it's so hard to eat healthy. It's a great question.

HEALTHY EATING only seems hard because we have been tricked into believing that things that look like food, that masquerade as food, and that are sold to us as food are actually not food (I hesitate to use the term "food" at all when I refer to these chemical-filled collages of artificial colors, flavors, and preservatives). For more than a century, these processed "phony foods" became the norm, while fresh, whole foods fell out of favor.

Phony foods first showed up in the nineteenth century and have been making their way onto our grocery store shelves, and into our bodies, ever since. They've been aggressively marketed to us by food manufacturers, large retail chains, and fast-food restaurants for decades. Factory farms have supplied an abundance of corn, soy, and wheat to fuel the creation of these products. In the fifties, so much corn was produced that the government and the food industry had to figure out how to use it. Their solution? Turn it into sugar, give it four hundred different names, and put it in 90 percent of all processed foods.

As a result, the food industry successfully hooked an entire population on sugar-laced and processed foods. They've made trillions of dollars, while their consumers have become obese and sick.

Luckily, there has been a backlash against phony foods in recent years. In addition to the rise in popularity of farmers' markets, the growing practice of producing foods sustainably, and an increased awareness among consumers that the quality and source of their food matters, people are also starting to embrace eating philosophies that reflect a desire to get back to basics.

One such philosophy is the plant-based eating movement. Now, I promised you that I wouldn't bore you with a bunch of diet dogma in this book, and I intend to keep that promise. I don't believe that you need to follow someone else's diet plan to be healthy. But I do believe that we all need to eat more nutrient-dense foods to be healthy, and plants are some of the most nutritious foods around.

People who adhere to a strictly plant-based eating regimen are usually known as vegans. Please don't close the book—I'm not asking you to become a vegan! I'm not asking you to give up meat, or even eggs. That's why this is a (mostly) plant-based cookbook—I don't advocate a strictly vegan or vegetarian diet. But I am asking you to go back to basics: to eat more of the things that are produced by Mother Nature and less of the things that are made in a factory.

So what does my version of *mostly* plant-based eating look like? Here are a few of the main points:

EAT MORE PLANTS

It's as simple as it sounds. The nutrients in fresh, organic vegetables and fruits (and other "living" foods such as sprouted seeds, nuts, grains, and beans) help our bodies to not only survive, but thrive. Aim to make vegetables the star of your meals, with meat playing a supporting role. Don't worry, that doesn't mean that you have to eat the same old salad or steamed broccoli every day. In this book you'll find plenty of recipes—such as Ajo Blanco (page 110), Radicchio Citrus Salad (page 125), Cauliflower Risotto (page 176), and Asian Veggie Burgers (page 163)—that will show you how to prepare fresh vegetables in totally new and delicious ways.

CONSUME MEAT IN MODERATION

There's nothing wrong with including some meat in your diet as long as you choose high-quality sources. Lean cuts of beef, chicken, turkey, and seafood are all great choices that provide iron, amino acids, and other important nutrients your body needs.

Always buy the best-quality animal protein you can afford. Look for organic, grass-fed meat labeled "American Grassfed Approved" or "USDA Process Verified Grass-fed." This certification guarantees that the animal was raised on a diet of 99 percent grass and had seasonal access to a pasture. Organic cattle are raised without routine treatment of antibiotics or hormones. Emerging research suggests that meat from organic grass-fed cattle might be healthier for us than animals fattened on a conventional diet of grain, or given antibiotics and hormones.

When it comes to poultry, opt for organic—chickens and turkeys with the "certified organic" label are almost always raised without the regular use of hormones and antibiotics. And organic birds can't be fed "poultry litter," which is a feed mixture that includes droppings (ick!).

There's no such thing as an organic farmed fish, although the USDA is looking into it. Organic fish would be raised in open-net pens in large bodies of water—a method that has drawn the ire of environmental groups that are concerned about water contamination. Until this issue gets sorted out, your best bet is to purchase and eat wild-caught fish. To me, it's logical that anything labeled "wild" is naturally organic!

DITCH THE DAIRY

Most chefs don't like to eliminate dairy from their recipes, but when I decided to take charge of my health, I spent a lot of time devising recipes to replace dairy in my cooking.

Dairy has an inflammatory effect in the body and packs a ton of calories, so I do my best to avoid it. I've spent a lot of time devising recipes that use nondairy milks, like coconut milk and almond milk, and you would never know the difference. In fact, I think these foods are superior in taste to regular dairy foods!

Every once in a while I use a little bit of Parmesan cheese in a recipe—because there is nothing like the taste of real Parmesan, and just a small amount of fresh grated cheese packs a lot of flavor. But for the most part, I cook with non-dairy cheeses, like cashew cheese or even "ricotta" made from almonds. Trust me, if anyone can make almond ricotta–stuffed chicken taste like the real thing, it's this Italian boy!

CHOOSE GLUTEN-FREE GRAINS

Gluten—which many consider toxic to the body—is a protein found in wheat and other grains such as barley and rye. It promotes chronic inflammation throughout the body if you're sensitive or allergic to it. Gluten also triggers leptin resistance. Leptin is a hormone that sends signals to the brain when you've eaten enough that you're full and don't want any more food. In other words, leptin keeps your hunger in check so you don't overeat. Leptin resistance can make you prone to overeating. Grains, especially the gluten-containing ones, are thought to promote leptin resistance and therefore weight gain and obesity.

Fortunately, it's easier than ever to avoid gluten; gluten-free flours made from legumes, ancient grains, and nuts are widely available. I love chickpea flour, for example. It rises quickly and is great for baked goods and coatings.

PLANTS IN THE RAW

While many of the recipes in this book require you to fire up your stove, I've also included plenty of raw foods, including meals and snacks that can be assembled quickly and no-bake desserts that are a breeze to throw together.

One reason I've included "raw" recipes is because they're so simple to assemble, and I want to make it as easy as possible for you to make your meals at home. But the other reason is because eating uncooked plants offers a range of health benefits. Here are just a few:

Better Digestion. Raw foods retain all of their enzymes, and enzymes help your body digest food. The body can create enzymes on its own, but that process uses up a lot of energy; that's one of the reasons you sometimes feel sluggish after eating a cooked meal. Further, the enzymes produced by the body are not as efficient and effective as the ones you obtain from food. Raw food is digested more easily, absorbed better, and eliminated more efficiently and regularly than cooked food. When you incorporate more raw food into your diet, your whole system starts operating as it should. You'll sleep better, maintain an ideal weight, and boost your immunity.

Beneficial pH. Your blood pH level fluctuates between alkalinity and acidity. When your blood is more alkaline than acidic, inflammation is reduced and your immune system is enhanced. A slightly alkaline pH level may also help you lose weight faster, because alkalinity helps to zap food cravings. Most raw fruits and vegetables are alkaline.

Heart Health. Diets focusing on raw fruits and vegetables have been studied sporadically over the years, and there's clinical proof of health benefits from going raw, particularly for your cardiovascular system. The *European Journal of Clinical Nutrition* reported in 2011 that a high intake of raw fruit and vegetables may even protect against stroke. And in one of the largest diet and heart studies ever conducted, researchers at McMaster and McGill universities in Canada found that people who ate a healthy diet composed mostly of raw fruits and vegetables dramatically weakened the effects of a gene that is implicated in heart disease.

Longevity. Eating raw vegetables and fruits may offer anti-aging benefits. Elderly Italians whose diet consisted mostly of raw vegetables and olive oil lived longer than Italians who ate mostly pasta and meat, according to a study reported in the *British Journal of Medicine* in 2010.

ARE RAW FOODS SAFE?

When you're eating raw food, you may be concerned about e-coli on spinach, salmonella, or parasites. You may think: "Is it really safe to eat raw food? I'm sure there must have been a reason why people started cooking their food."

Before refrigeration, cooking food was considered the only way to kill parasites and bacteria. Then, Louis Pasteur developed pasteurization—a food-safety technique that destroys pathogens by heat. However, this method has numerous disadvantages. It doesn't just kill the bad bacteria, it also kills the good ones, along with the food's enzymes. In addition, heating food causes it to become more acidic and can reduce the amount of vitamins and minerals present. Today, we have much better methods for keeping our food safe, including refrigeration and vacuum sealing. Of course, always clean your fresh produce thoroughly under cool running water (even if organic) to make sure any contaminants are washed away.

EASY WAYS TO EAT MORE RAW FOODS

- Aim to eat at least one salad a day.
- Snack on raw fruit, vegetables, nuts, and seeds.
- Sprinkle sprouts on your salad or add them to a sandwich. Sprouts from foods such as mung beans, chickpeas, lentils, adzuki beans, alfalfa seeds, radish seeds, mustard seeds, and millet are all brimming with live enzymes and some are high in protein.

- Fire up your blender and make fresh veggie soups that can be served cold, like my Ajo Blanco (page 110) or Cauliflower Soup (page 108).
- Juice raw vegetables. Fresh vegetable juices are concentrated sources of nutrients—just be careful not to add in high-sugar fruit juice. A little lemon and ginger will work wonders.

If you're going to be upping your intake of fruits and vegetables, it's important to pay attention to the quality of your produce. In the next chapter, we'll take a closer look at what "organic" really means and why you shouldn't settle for anything less.

CREATING A PLANT-BASED PANTRY

Here's a list of must-have items to begin creating healthy and delicious plant-based meals. There are a number of other ingredients you'll find in my recipes, but these fifteen should be your staples.

1. ALTERNATIVE FLOURS.

To keep everything gluten-free, have on hand the following flours: almond flour, a heart-healthy, higher protein flour that is also good if you're following a low-carb diet; buckwheat flour, an excellent source of minerals; and hazelnut flour, another low-carb flour that has a sweet, nutty flavor.

2. BALSAMIC VINEGAR.

I love cooking with this vinegar because its sweet-tart, wood-aged taste makes it a great flavor enhancer. There's a lot you can do with it: Use it in salad dressings, in marinades, on meats, and with veggies. You can even boil it down until it reduces to a thick consistency that can then be used as a sauce base.

3. BEANS.

One of the superfoods in plant-based cooking, beans pack a lot of protein and fiber. It's perfectly fine to use canned beans; they'll save you time in the kitchen. Stock up on cans of black beans, cannellini beans, kidney beans, chickpeas, and red beans.

4. CHIA SEEDS.

Have a bag or two of these omega-3, fiber-rich seeds in your pantry. They're wonderful in smoothies, puddings, and cereals.

5. CHOCOLATE.

In truth, chocolate is a health food, full of antioxidants. This cookbook gives you nearly thirty recipes that include chocolate, from cookies to puddings to candies. My secret to creating luscious, healthy chocolate recipes is using cocoa powder and chocolate chips. Both lend chocolatey goodness and flavor to desserts, but without even a chocolate-chip-size morsel of guilt.

6. COCONUT NECTAR.

This sweetener is made from the sweet juice that drips off coconut flower buds. It, too, contains nutrients not found in refined sugars: seventeen amino acids, as well as a bunch of minerals and vitamins B and C. Granulated coconut nectar has a caramel/maple flavor and can be used in place of brown sugar in recipes. I love it on top of fruit or toast and in hot cereals or for baking.

7. COCONUT YOGURT & COCONUT MILK.

Because I rarely cook with dairy products anymore, my go-to alternatives are unsweetened coconut yogurt and coconut milk. Either one can replace cream or milk in a recipe at almost a one-to-one swap. Coconut with its natural sweetness is one of the ingredients that turns healthy food into delicious food. (Neither of these are pantry items; they must be refrigerated. I listed them here because they're called for in many of my recipes.)

8. HEMP HEARTS.

This versatile seed has an amazing flavor and can be used for a lot more than just topping salads. When you add hemp hearts to a plant-based dish, it intensifies and brings out the earthy flavor. It will do the same to meat dishes; it amplifies the meaty taste. Bottom line: Hemp seeds are rich in healthy fats and essential fatty acids. They are also a great protein source and contain high amounts of vitamin E, phosphorus, potassium, sodium, magnesium, sulfur, calcium, iron, and zinc.

9. MONK FRUIT.

This sweetener is made from a small green melon called a monk fruit. It's been cultivated in Asia for hundreds of years and supposedly got its name from Buddhist monks who grew the fruit in southern China. Today the fruit is crushed, mixed with hot water, filtered, and spray-dried to form a sweet, zero-calorie powder, now used in a number of foods and beverages, from granola to cocktails. Monk fruit is three hundred times sweeter than sugar, and you can cook with it.

10. OILS.

I use several different oils for the recipes here. Of course, my standard is extra-virgin olive oil. Extra-virgin means the oil is the product of the very first pressing of the olives; it simply tastes better than any other pressing. The other oils I use are: sesame oil, a rich and nutty oil used in Asian-inspired dishes; coconut oil, a "super oil" with many medicinal and culinary benefits; hazelnut oil, a food staple of the heart-healthy Mediterranean diet; and grapeseed oil, pressed from the seeds of grapes and a great source of antioxidants and vitamin E.

11. PROTEIN POWDER.

You'll find your fill of delicious smoothies here, so you'll want to have a good protein powder on hand to pump up your protein. Look for one that is plant-protein-based or egg-based, and free of sugar, dairy, fat, and soy.

12. PUFFED BROWN RICE.

This cereal is low in calories, fat-free, sodium-free, and gluten-free. I use it as a healthy filler for many dishes, rather than breadcrumbs, and it performs beautifully.

13. QUINOA.

Here is the most popular gluten-free grain you can eat (although it is really a seed). Quinoa is loaded with protein and is one of the few plant foods containing all nine essential amino acids. Plus, it tastes heavenly in salads, as a filler for burgers, and as a side dish accented with herbs.

14. ROLLED OATS.

Make sure you're well-stocked with rolled oats. They're higher in protein and lower in carbs than most other grains. Plus, they are the only source of a certain type of antioxidant that protects arteries from clogging.

15. STEVIA.

I've used stevia in its powdered and liquid forms for a long time and with good results. This sweetener is extracted from a South American herb and is estimated to be as much as four hundred times sweeter than sugar. It has no calories and can be used safely by people with diabetes without raising blood sugar or impacting glucose levels. To bake with it, use 1½ tablespoons powdered (or 1 teaspoon liquid) stevia for 1 cup sugar. It takes some experimentation to achieve the right sweetness.

CHAPTER 3

10 Reasons to Go Organic

Like any chef, I'm always on the hunt for high-quality food; when you cook with the best ingredients, it's easy to make delicious meals. And on the whole, I believe that organic foods offer superior flavor. But I also cook with organic foods because I want to feed myself and others in the healthiest way possible.

THE TERM "organic" refers to the practice of planting and harvesting crops in sync with the cycles of nature and without the use of herbicides, fungicides, pesticides, or synthetic fertilizers—basically, the way food used to be grown before factory farms took over agriculture and poisoned our food supply with toxic chemicals.

The U.S. Department of Agriculture (USDA) has established standards for organic food production. In order to be certified organic, a food must be produced without the use of:

- Antibiotics
- Artificial growth hormones
- High-fructose corn syrup
- Artificial dyes (made from coal tar and petrochemicals)
- Artificial sweeteners derived from chemicals
- Synthetically created chemical pesticides and fertilizers
- Genetically engineered proteins and ingredients
- Sewage sludge (see below)
- Irradiation (zapping food with high-energy rays to kill microorganisms)

Choosing organic foods is important when it comes to plant-based eating. Let's dig a little deeper into the rationale for going organic now.

1. YOU WON'T BE INGESTING HUMAN WASTE.

The Environmental Protection Agency (EPA) allows conventional farmers to use human waste ("human sludge") as fertilizer. Yes, you read that correctly. It's legal to dump people-poop fertilizer on farmland—a process being undertaken across the country by cities and towns that dispose of tons of waste daily after we flush our toilets.

Is this practice safe? No. Scientists analyzing the issue claim that human-waste fertilizers contain dangerous germs and heavy metals such as arsenic, cadmium, chromium, lead, selenium, and mercury. These potentially hazardous substances are not found in livestock manure.

So if you just want one compelling factor to go organic, know that organic foods are not fertilized with human sludge. Now you know the truth.

2. YOU WON'T BE EATING PESTICIDES.

I love strawberries. Give me a bowl of big, sweet, and juicy berries with an overwhelming strawberry-ness that spurts a little juice down my chin, and I'm in heaven.

But if those strawberries are not organic, I've got trouble in my bowl. Turns out that there are forty-five pesticide residues on conventionally grown strawberries, according to a USDA pesticide data program. Six of these residues are known or probable carcinogens. Sixteen are suspected hormone disruptors. This means they act like estrogen in the body and disrupt natural thyroid hormones, which regulate metabolism.

Seven are neurotoxins and thus harmful to the brain, thinking skills, and memory. Six cause developmental or reproductive issues, and twelve are environmental toxins, which do things like kill honeybees. (To find out how many pesticide residues are on your favorite foods, check out the website www.whatsonmyfood.org.)

If it's not organic, this wonderful berry, which is full of fiber and antioxidants and low in sugar, is in reality a little nugget of poison.

3. YOU'LL SUPERCHARGE YOUR BODY WITH NUTRIENTS.

You'll come across information that claims the opposite, that conventionally grown food is more nutritious than organic food, but don't believe it. One of the most eye-opening studies on this issue was published in the *British Journal of Nutrition*. It was a "meta-analysis" (statistical study) of 343 peer-reviewed publications that looked into significant and meaningful differences in nutrients between organic and conventionally grown crops. Compared to nonorganic crops, the study concluded that organic fruits and vegetables:

- Contain higher concentrations of a range of disease-preventing antioxidants.

- Are higher in vitamin C, a nutrient important for practically every system in the body, from skin to heart.

- Have higher amounts of magnesium and zinc. Found in almost every cell in the body, magnesium serves a vital role in most of the body's biological activities. Zinc is also involved in the metabolism of fats, protein, and carbohydrates, among other duties.

- Contain higher levels of carotenoids, nutrients that, among other health benefits, reduce the risk of degenerative diseases and cancer.

- Have higher concentrations of lutein, a valuable carotenoid in fruits and vegetables that helps protect against heart disease and some cancers, and has been shown to reduce the risk of eye problems, such as cataracts and macular degeneration.

4. YOUR FOOD WILL TASTE BETTER.

There haven't been a lot of studies done on whether organic food tastes better than conventionally grown food, so I've had to apply my own test, the Rocco Taste Test. When I started cooking with, and eating, organic foods, I couldn't believe the superior flavor of organic produce and pasture-fed, responsibly raised meats.

With organic ingredients, you don't need to add a lot of extra flavoring. If you already purchase organic food, you know that there is a depth of flavor, improved texture, and quality to these ingredients that simply does not exist in much of the mass-produced food of today.

5. YOU CAN EAT ORGANIC WITHOUT GOING BROKE.

Admittedly, organic food can be a little pricey sometimes. Why should you have to pay more for organically grown foods? Without getting too much into the politics of it, the government makes it a lot harder for organic farmers to turn a profit than the factory farms that use pesticides. I believe that real food, without antibiotics, growth hormones, and excessive pesticide residue, should be a basic human right, afforded to all of us, no matter what our socioeconomic status. But until things change, we've got to make some budget adjustments at home and in the grocery store.

One easy way to get organic food at a lower price is to visit your local farmers' market. If you go to the market shortly before closing time, you may not get the pick of the litter, but the farmers are usually willing to offer discounts or negotiate prices to get some of the produce off their hands.

Some other tips for buying organic at budget-friendly prices:

- Stock up and buy in bulk when possible; bulk is always cheaper.

- Shop at places like Walmart, Target, or Costco; you can find organic foods at very low prices without having to go to more expensive natural foods stores.

- Make shopping lists to guide your food purchases in a healthy direction and to avoid impulse buying.

- Clip coupons and consult your supermarket flyers to find food bargains. The Supplemental Nutrition Assistance Program (SNAP) issues electronic benefits that can be used like cash to purchase food. SNAP helps low-income working people, senior citizens, the disabled, and others feed their families.

- Make use of savings techniques at the supermarket, such as using discount cards or cash-back deals like Walmart's Savings Catcher.

- Let your local, state, and federal legislators know that you believe organic food should be the affordable option to families. They have family members struggling under the burden of disease. As the science continues to mount, it's shocking to me to learn just how much the food we eat—and the artificial ingredients being added to it—is harming our health and the health of our loved ones. Becoming an advocate for safer, healthier food is one of the most patriotic things that we can do.

Finally, let me emphasize that while it may cost a little more to buy organic foods, it is infinitely more expensive to be unhealthy. Have you priced a bypass surgery lately?

6. YOU'LL PREPARE SAFE, HEALTHFUL FOOD FOR YOUR CHILDREN.

When I learned that the average baby is born with two hundred toxins and carcinogens in its body, I was stunned. Further, by the time kids reach age two, most have exceeded the lethal limit for the toxins. All of this really hit a nerve with me. Feed your kids organic food, and those toxins will drop or be nonexistent. Organic food means healthier children.

7. YOU'LL AVOID IRRADIATED FOODS.

I always wondered why the organic vegetables and fruits I bought seemed to spoil so much faster than nonorganic produce. I looked into this issue and discovered the reason: Many foods are irradiated. Irradiation kills bacteria and extends the shelf life of food. There's more: It also alters the food's molecular structure. That's because some irradiation uses radioactive substances; others employ high-energy electrons or X-rays. I don't know about you, but I prefer my food pure and not radioactively zapped—and that means going organic.

8. YOU WON'T INGEST GMOs.

Organic food is not genetically modified (GM) food. In a process that is totally unnatural, GMOs are made when genetic engineers insert genes from one living thing (say, a bacteria or a virus) into the DNA of a completely unrelated living thing (say, corn), in order to create a food product that is more tolerant to frost or weed killers, resistant to pests, or more shelf stable.

Scientists from our own Food and Drug Administration (FDA) cautioned that GM foods could give rise to new toxins and new allergens and need more rigorous testing, but their warnings went largely unheeded. Instead, the US government officially stated that GM foods are "substantially equivalent" to conventional foods and they don't need safety testing or labeling. This position is the exact opposite of what forty other countries do—and that is to mandate GM labeling on foods.

I object to GM foods—I know you saw that coming—mainly because I want to protect my health. The American Academy of Environmental Medicine (AAEM) has enumerated the potential health risks posed by eating GM foods: infertility, weakened immunity, accelerated aging, poor insulin control, abnormal cholesterol, and gastrointestinal issues, among others.

Our government continues to be secretive—at least vague—about these health consequences. I've read enough to not want to take a chance. Do you?

9. YOU'LL PROMOTE THE HUMANE TREATMENT OF ANIMALS.

Organic animal farms treat their livestock much more humanely—no pens, cages, or unnatural feed or diets—than conventional farms. As an animal lover, this is reason enough for me to choose organically raised meat and poultry.

10. YOU'LL HELP SAVE THE ENVIRONMENT.

Buying organic food has a positive impact on the environment—in two major ways. First, conventional farming methods erode soil and use dangerous pesticides that seep into the soil and can stay there for centuries. A good example is the pesticide DDT, once thought to be harmless but now known to be extremely toxic to health. Even though this pesticide has been banned for many years now, traces are still detectable in virtually all bodies of water, our bodies, and in animals around the world.

Second, nonorganic animal food (meat, fish,

dairy, and eggs) is polluting the environment. According to research, animal food contributes to as much as 95 percent of the toxic chemical residues in the American diet, including residues from pesticides such as DDT, DDE, and TDE.

Hopefully by now I've convinced you to choose organic whenever possible. I don't expect you to be perfect—sometimes you just can't find the organic version of a certain ingredient, or it might be too expensive for your budget. That's fine. Plant-based eating isn't about becoming the healthiest person in the world, it's about being a healthier version of yourself. The most important thing is to choose real foods over phony foods; to fill your plate with vegetables; to incorporate more raw foods into your life; and to get into the kitchen as much as possible.

Oh, and one last thing: We're going to have fun and eat some delicious food along the way. Now, let's get cooking!

PART II
The Recipes

CHAPTER 4

Morning

PROTEIN PANCAKES

MAKES FOUR 6-INCH PANCAKES

These are the high-protein, gluten-free pancakes you've been searching for—they are one of the most popular items among my clients. I've replaced the fat with applesauce, a healthy sub for fat in baked goods that also imparts a hint of sweetness with no added sugar.

PREP TIME: 5 MINUTES
COOK TIME: 10 MINUTES

INGREDIENTS

½   cup unsweetened applesauce
2   eggs
1   teaspoon baking powder
1   scoop protein powder
     (such as Rocco's Protein Powder Plus)

METHOD

1. In a small bowl, whisk together the applesauce, eggs, baking powder, and protein powder until just combined.
2. Heat a 6-inch nonstick skillet over medium heat. Coat with cooking spray and pour 3 ounces of batter into the pan.
3. Cook until the edges of the pancake are set, about 45 seconds. Flip and cook another 15 to 30 seconds. Repeat to make 3 more pancakes. Serve with Blueberry Syrup.

PER SERVING
77 calories / 2.5g fat (1g sat) / 8g protein
6g carbohydrates / 2.5g fiber

BLUEBERRY SYRUP

MAKES 4 SERVINGS

It only takes 5 minutes to whip up this luscious blueberry syrup. It has a fraction of the calories of maple syrup and packs the antioxidant power of blueberries, making it just about the healthiest breakfast syrup you'll find.

PREP TIME: 5 MINUTES
COOK TIME: 5 MINUTES

INGREDIENTS

1   pint blueberries
5   packets Monk Fruit in the Raw

METHOD

1. Place the blueberries in a small pot and cook over medium heat until they soften and begin to burst, about 5 minutes.
2. Transfer the berries to a blender, add the monk fruit, and puree until smooth, 15 to 30 seconds.

Tip: The syrup will thicken as it cools. Warm it up to get it back to its liquid state before serving.

PER SERVING
43 calories / <0.5g fat / <1g protein
11g carbohydrates / 2g fiber

PROTEIN CREPES

MAKES 4 SERVINGS OF THREE 6-INCH CREPES

Crepes are a type of very thin pancake. Though usually made from wheat flour, mine use buckwheat flour to make them gluten-free. The word "crepe" derives from the Latin *crispa*, meaning "curled"—which is what the edges of the crepes should look like as they finish cooking. Adding protein powder pumps up the protein content, along with the liquid egg whites. You can serve these with any type of sweet or savory filling—I love using fresh pureed berries.

PREP TIME: 5 MINUTES
COOK TIME: 10 MINUTES

INGREDIENTS

1 **cup liquid egg whites**

½ **cup unsweetened applesauce**

1 **scoop protein powder (such as Rocco's Protein Powder Plus)**

2 **tablespoons buckwheat flour**

METHOD

1. In a small bowl, gently whisk together the egg whites, applesauce, protein powder, and buckwheat flour until just combined.

2. Place a 6-inch nonstick skillet over medium heat. Coat with cooking spray and add a heaping tablespoon of batter to the pan, swirling to coat the bottom evenly. Cook until the edges of the crepe begin to curl slightly, about 30 seconds. Flip and cook an additional 15 seconds.

3. Repeat until you have 12 crepes.

PER SERVING (THREE CREPES)
86 calories / <0.5g fat / 12g protein
9g carbohydrates / 3g fiber

FRUITY COCO YOGURT SWIRL

MAKES 4 SERVINGS

―――――――――

PREP TIME: 5 MINUTES
COOK TIME: 5 MINUTES

INGREDIENTS

1½ cups strawberries, quartered

2 cups unsweetened nondairy coconut yogurt (such as So Delicious)

8 packets Monk Fruit in the Raw

¼ cup raw almonds, chopped

METHOD

1. Place the strawberries in a small saucepan and cook until they become soft and start to break apart, about 5 minutes.

2. If you like your yogurt toppings smooth, puree in a blender for 30 seconds. If you like them chunkier, break the strawberries against the side of the pan with a silicone spatula.

3. In a small bowl, combine the yogurt and monk fruit.

4. Spoon the yogurt into serving bowls and top with the berries. Swirl them into the yogurt by stirring a couple of times with a spoon. Add the almonds.

PER SERVING
227 calories / 7g fat / 2g protein / 11g carbohydrates / 4g fiber

EGG AND PANCAKE SANDWICH

MAKES 4 SERVINGS

What do you get when you put perfectly cooked eggs between two pancakes? A little slice of breakfast sandwich heaven. This is a tasty, protein-rich, deceptively healthy—and very delicious—way to start your day.

PREP TIME: 20 MINUTES
COOK TIME: 10 MINUTES

INGREDIENTS

½   cup unsweetened applesauce
6   eggs
1   teaspoon baking powder
1   scoop protein powder
    (such as Rocco's Protein Powder Plus)
1   tablespoon raw coconut nectar

METHOD

1. In a small bowl, mix the applesauce, 2 of the eggs, the baking powder, and protein powder with a fork until just combined.

2. Heat a large nonstick skillet over medium heat and coat the pan with cooking spray. Cook 8 silver dollar–size pancakes until the edges are just set and bubbles begin to form in the pancakes, about 90 seconds. Flip the pancakes and cook another 30 to 45 seconds.

3. In the same pan, cook the remaining 4 eggs over-easy. Place an egg on each of 4 pancakes and top with the remaining pancakes. Drizzle the coconut nectar on top and allow it to absorb for 1 minute before eating.

PER SERVING
162 calories / 7g fat / 15g protein
9g carbohydrates / 2.5g fiber

TOAD-IN-THE-HOLE

MAKES 4 SERVINGS

———

When I started making gluten-free baked goods, I discovered that buckwheat is surprisingly perfect for the task and makes a delicious bread. The "toad" here is the egg, baked into holes cut into the bread.

PREP TIME: 10 MINUTES
COOK TIME: 40 MINUTES

INGREDIENTS

⅓ cup buckwheat flour

½ teaspoon baking powder
   Salt

5 eggs

2 tablespoons unsweetened coconut milk beverage (such as So Delicious)

6 ounces smoked salmon

¼ cup chopped dill

METHOD

1. Preheat the oven to 350°F.
2. In a small bowl, use a fork to combine the buckwheat flour, baking powder, salt, 1 of the eggs, and the coconut milk.
3. Coat an 8½ by 4½-inch loaf pan with a thin layer of olive oil or coconut oil. Place the dough into the loaf pan. Bake until a toothpick inserted into the center of the loaf comes out dry, about 30 minutes.
4. Slice the bread into 4 slices and cut a hole in the center of each slice. Place on a baking sheet.
5. Crack an egg into each hole. Season with salt and transfer to the oven. Bake until the white of the egg is set, about 10 minutes.
6. Serve with the salmon on the side and sprinkled with the dill.

Tip: Bake the bread the night before. It will be waiting for you in the morning.

PER SERVING
178 calories / 8g fat / 19g protein
0g carbohydrate / 1.5g fiber

SHAKSHUKA

MAKES 4 SERVINGS

———————

When I say we're having *shakshuka* for breakfast, my friends hand me a tissue because they think I just sneezed. If you've never heard of shakshuka, you're in for a treat. It's basically eggs poached in a rich tomato-based sauce. In Israel, it's typically eaten for breakfast, but it works well for brunch, lunch, even dinner. My recipe includes a spice called *ras el hanout*, a spice mix from North Africa, consisting of a mixture of cardamom, cloves, cinnamon, allspice, chile peppers, and more.

PREP TIME: 10 MINUTES
COOK TIME: 30 MINUTES

INGREDIENTS

2   cups thinly sliced white onions

1½ cups thinly sliced red bell peppers

2   cloves garlic, sliced

1   teaspoon ras el hanout

4   cups chopped tomatoes

4   eggs

¼   cup cilantro, whole leaves

METHOD

1. Preheat the oven to 375°F.

2. Place a 12-inch cast-iron skillet over high heat for 4 minutes, until hot. Add the onions and bell peppers and cook until softened, about 10 minutes. Add the garlic and *ras el hanout* and cook another 2 minutes. Add the tomatoes and cook until they break down and the sauce becomes thick, 10 to 12 minutes.

3. Crack the eggs into the mixture. Transfer the pan to the oven and bake until the eggs are just set, 7 to 10 minutes. Top with the cilantro and serve immediately.

Tip: You will want to keep your favorite hot sauce at hand to serve with this recipe.

PER SERVING
141 calories / 21g fat / 9g protein
16g carbohydrates / 4g fiber

EGGS FLORENTINE

MAKES 4 SERVINGS

Just about any food put atop spinach is called Florentine, a style of dish that was named for the birthplace (Florence, Italy) of Catherine de Medici, who introduced the leafy green into Gallic cuisine when she married France's Prince Henry in 1533. Here's the classic dish, turned into a healthy, delicious, and low-carb breakfast.

PREP TIME: 10 MINUTES
COOK TIME: 15 MINUTES

INGREDIENTS

1   tablespoon extra-virgin olive oil
½   small onion, finely chopped
1   clove garlic, finely chopped
10 ounces spinach
¼   cup unsweetened nondairy coconut yogurt (such as So Delicious)
1   tablespoon lemon juice
4   eggs
4   slices tomato (½ inch thick)

METHOD

1. Warm the olive oil in a large skillet over medium heat. Add the onion and sweat until soft, about 5 minutes. Add the garlic and cook another 3 minutes. Add the spinach and cook until wilted, 2 to 3 minutes.
2. Remove from the heat. Stir in the coconut yogurt and lemon juice. Set aside.
3. Fill a sauté pan with 1½ inches water and bring to a bare simmer. Gently stir the water with a spoon to create a whirlpool. Crack the eggs in one at a time and cook about 3 minutes to poach. Remove with a slotted spoon and drain on a paper towel.
4. To plate, place 1 slice of tomato on a plate. Top with the spinach and place the egg on top.

Tips: Add a couple of tablespoons of distilled vinegar to your poaching water. This helps the egg white better coagulate and makes poaching easier. Garnish with black pepper or red chile flakes if you wish.

PER SERVING
143 calories / 9g fat / 9g protein
8g carbohydrates / 3g fiber

EGGPLANT AND TURKEY BACON HASH

MAKES 4 SERVINGS

Here's a one-dish breakfast that serves up practically every vital nutrient on the planet—antioxidants, phytochemicals, vitamins, minerals, good fats, protein, carbs, and more. And that's just the nutrition. Wait until you put the first savory bite in your mouth. You'll be clamoring for this dish every morning!

PREP TIME: 20 MINUTES
COOK TIME: 30 MINUTES

INGREDIENTS

4 cups chopped, unpeeled eggplant
   Salt
1 tablespoon extra-virgin olive oil
2 cups chopped onions
½ cup chopped green bell pepper
2 cups peeled, chopped sweet potato
2 slices turkey bacon, chopped
2 eggs

METHOD

1. Preheat the oven to 375°F.
2. Line a rimmed baking sheet with paper towels. Place the eggplant on the sheet and lightly salt it. Let sit for about 20 minutes, then press the moisture out of it.
3. Heat the olive oil in a large cast-iron pan over medium heat. Add the onions, bell pepper, and sweet potato and cook until the onions are translucent and the bell pepper and sweet potatoes are soft, about 10 minutes.
4. Increase the heat to high and add the turkey bacon and eggplant. Cook until the eggplant is browned, about 5 minutes. Gently turn the hash and cook another 5 minutes to brown the other side.
5. Crack the eggs on top and move to the oven to bake until the egg white is set, 7 to 8 minutes.

PER SERVING
190 calories / 8g fat / 8g protein
23g carbohydrates / 7g fiber

TURMERIC, ENGLISH PEA, AND ONION FRITTATA

MAKES 4 SERVINGS

To this day, one of my favorite foods is my mom's frittata, an egg-based Italian dish similar to an omelet or crustless quiche. This one is deliciously vegetarian and spiced with turmeric, a healing anti-inflammatory ingredient. I love making frittatas because they're easier and faster than omelets. If you want a great brunch recipe, whip up this high-protein meal that will keep your whole family full and energized.

PREP TIME: 5 MINUTES
COOK TIME: 15 MINUTES

INGREDIENTS

1   cup sliced red onion

⅔   cup frozen peas, thawed

1   tablespoon finely grated fresh turmeric

4   eggs, beaten

METHOD

1. Preheat the oven to 325°F.
2. Heat a 6-inch nonstick ovenproof skillet over medium heat. Add the red onion and sweat until soft, about 7 minutes. Add the peas and cook for 3 minutes. Add the turmeric and eggs and stir with a silicone spatula until about half-set.
3. Move the pan to the oven and bake until the eggs are cooked, 7 to 10 minutes.

PER SERVING
96 calories / 5g fat / 7g protein
6g carbohydrates / 1g fiber

SWEET POTATO, BELL PEPPER, AND ONION TORTILLA

MAKES 4 SERVINGS

The Spanish *tortilla* is a hearty dish made from potatoes, spices, and any variety of additional ingredients such as veggies, cheese, or meat. In my version I've loaded it up with vitamin C–rich bell peppers and flavored it with onions. This dish is delicious served hot or cold.

PREP TIME: 10 MINUTES
COOK TIME: 20 MINUTES

INGREDIENTS

2   cups very thinly sliced sweet potatoes (See Tip)

½   cup sliced yellow onion

¾   cup sliced green bell pepper

4   eggs, beaten

¼   cup chopped Italian flat parsley

METHOD

1. Preheat the oven to 325°F.
2. Place the sweet potatoes on a microwave-safe plate.
3. Heat a nonstick ovenproof skillet over medium heat. Add the onion and bell pepper and sweat until soft and translucent, about 10 minutes.
4. When the onions and peppers are almost soft, put the sweet potatoes in the microwave for 2 minutes to soften them, then add to the pan with the vegetables.
5. Add the eggs and parsley and stir with a silicone spatula until the eggs are slightly set.
6. Place in the oven for 5 minutes. Remove from the oven and flip the tortilla out onto a plate. Return it to the pan and bake for another 5 minutes.
7. To serve, flip the tortilla out onto a plate and cut into 4 pieces.

Tip: If you have a mandoline, slicing the potatoes will be a breeze, but watch your fingers!

PER SERVING
105 calories / 5g fat / 7g protein
8g carbohydrates / 1g fiber

MICROWAVE BUCKWHEAT BREAD

MAKES 4 SERVINGS (2 SLICES EACH)

PREP TIME: 3 MINUTES
COOK TIME: 2 MINUTES

INGREDIENTS

⅔ cup buckwheat flour
1 teaspoon baking powder
 Pinch of salt
2 eggs
¼ cup unsweetened lite coconut milk

METHOD

1. Coat two coffee mugs with cooking spray.
2. In a small bowl, mix the buckwheat flour, baking powder, and salt with a fork. Add the eggs and coconut milk and continue to mix with the fork.
3. Divide the mixture evenly between the coffee mugs and microwave until a toothpick inserted in the center of a bread comes out clean, about 90 seconds. Turn out, slice, and eat.

Tip: This bread toasts up like any other bread, either in a toaster oven or a pan.

PER SERVING
104 calories / 13g fat / 6g protein
14g carbohydrates / <1g fiber

PROTEIN BREAD

MAKES 4 SERVINGS

PREP TIME: 5 MINUTES
COOK TIME: 20 MINUTES

INGREDIENTS

⅓ cup buckwheat flour
1 scoop Rocco's Protein Baking Mix or your favorite baking mix (such as Bob's Red Mill)
1 teaspoon baking powder
 Pinch of salt
2 eggs
¼ cup unsweetened coconut milk beverage (such as So Delicious)

METHOD

1. Preheat the oven to 350°F.
2. In a medium bowl, whisk together the buckwheat flour, baking mix, baking powder, and salt. Whisk in the eggs and coconut milk.
3. Pour the batter into a 5¾ x 3-inch mini loaf pan. Bake until a toothpick inserted into the center of the loaf comes out clean, 20 to 30 minutes. Remove from the pan and place on a wire rack to cool before slicing.

Tip: This recipe also works great in a toaster oven.

PER SERVING
100 calories / 3g fat / 9g protein
9g carbohydrates / 3g fiber

BREAKFAST REUBEN

MAKES 4 SERVINGS

Legend has it that Reuben Kulakofsky, a Jewish-Lithuanian grocer in Omaha, Nebraska, invented the Reuben sandwich to serve at weekly poker games around 1920. My rendition uses the traditional flavors of pastrami and sauerkraut, but replaces the usual corned beef with turkey breast for a healthier protein choice. Sauerkraut is not only tasty, it's also rich in gut-friendly probiotics, which have been shown to help boost immunity and aid in weight loss. Make your own bread—and in the microwave? Yes, you can do it! This recipe is simple, quick, and, of course, gluten-free.

PREP TIME: 5 MINUTES

INGREDIENTS

⅔ cup buckwheat flour

1 teaspoon baking powder

Salt to taste

2 eggs

6 ounces sliced pastrami-seasoned turkey breast

4 tablespoons sauerkraut

METHOD

1. Coat a round microwave-safe container with cooking spray.

2. In a small bowl, use a fork to combine the buckwheat flour, baking powder, salt, and eggs. Transfer the mixture to the container and microwave until a toothpick inserted into the bread comes out clean, about 90 seconds.

3. Let sit in the container for a few minutes to set. Turn out and slice into 8 pieces. Toast if desired.

4. Place the turkey breast and sauerkraut on 4 pieces of bread and top with the remaining pieces.

PER SERVING
148 calories / 4g fat / 15g protein
15g carbohydrates / 3g fiber

BACON, EGG, AND CHEESE BREAKFAST SANDWICH

MAKES 4 SERVINGS

Your favorite drive-through breakfast sandwich gets a healthy and delicious makeover here. It's gluten-free, dairy-free, and definitely guilt-free. It's free of just about everything except flavor.

PREP TIME: 10 MINUTES
COOK TIME: 20 MINUTES

INGREDIENTS

4 slices turkey bacon
⅔ cup buckwheat flour
1 teaspoon baking powder
  Pinch of salt
6 eggs
4 slices dairy-free cheese

METHOD

1. Cook the turkey bacon according to the package directions.
2. Coat a round microwave-safe container with cooking spray.
3. In a small bowl, use a fork to combine the buckwheat flour, baking powder, and 2 of the eggs. Transfer to the container and microwave until a toothpick inserted into the bread comes out clean, about 90 seconds.
4. Let sit in the container for a few minutes to set. Turn out and slice into 8 pieces.
5. Place a nonstick skillet over medium-low heat. Whisk together the remaining 4 eggs. Add to the pan and gently stir with a silicone spatula the entire time the eggs are cooking. Remove from the heat before the eggs become completely dry and rubbery, about 3 minutes.
6. Toast the slices of bread either in a toaster or in a dry skillet over medium heat.
7. Equally divide the eggs among 4 slices of bread. Place a slice of bacon on each egg, and top each with a slice of cheese. Finish the sandwiches by putting the remaining 4 slices of bread on top of the cheese.

PER SERVING
285 calories / 15g fat / 16g protein
18g carbohydrates / 2.5g fiber

KALE AND EGG BREAKFAST SANDWICH

MAKES 4 SERVINGS

———

Breakfast offers the perfect opportunity to pack more veggies into your day, and this tasty sandwich features the superstar green, kale. I've chosen the baby version of kale because it's slightly sweeter and less bitter than its grown-up counterpart.

PREP TIME: 5 MINUTES
COOK TIME: 15 MINUTES

INGREDIENTS

⅔ cup buckwheat flour
1 teaspoon baking powder
   Pinch of salt
6 eggs
1 tablespoon extra-virgin olive oil
10 ounces baby kale
   Pepper

METHOD

1. Coat a round microwave-safe container with cooking spray.
2. In a small bowl, use a fork to combine the buckwheat flour, baking powder, salt, and 2 of the eggs. Transfer to the container and microwave until a toothpick inserted into the bread comes out clean, about 90 seconds.
3. Let sit in the container for a few minutes to set. Turn out and slice into 8 pieces.
4. Heat the olive oil in a skillet over medium heat. When the oil is warm, add the kale and cook until just wilted, about 2 minutes.
5. Place a nonstick skillet over medium-low heat. Whisk together the remaining 4 eggs. Add to the pan and gently stir with a silicone spatula the entire time the eggs are cooking. Remove from the heat before the eggs become completely dry and rubbery, about 3 minutes.
6. Toast the slices of bread either in a toaster or in a dry skillet over medium heat. Sandwich the kale and eggs between 2 pieces of bread. Season to taste with pepper.

Tip: Add some garlic to your kale for an extra punch of flavor.

PER SERVING
238 calories / 12g fat / 14g protein
21g carbohydrates / 4g fiber

FRUITY ALMOND AND CHIA SANDWICH

MAKES 4 SERVINGS

———————

PREP TIME: 15 MINUTES
COOK TIME: 2 MINUTES

INGREDIENTS

- ⅔ cup almond meal/flour
- 1 teaspoon baking powder
  Pinch of salt
- 2 eggs
- ¼ cup unsweetened coconut milk beverage (such as So Delicious)
- 1 tablespoon hydrated chia seeds (see tip on page 98)
- 2 medium Bartlett pears, sliced
- ¼ cup raw almonds, chopped

METHOD

1. In a small bowl, combine the almond meal, baking powder, salt, eggs, and coconut milk with a fork.
2. Coat a microwave-safe glass with cooking spray. Transfer the dough to the glass and microwave until a toothpick inserted into the bread comes out clean, about 90 seconds. Allow to sit in the glass for a few minutes to set. Turn out and slice into 8 pieces.
3. Toast the sliced bread. Rub with the hydrated chia seeds. Top with the sliced pears and chopped almonds.

PER SERVING
248 calories / 17g fat / 10g protein
19g carbohydrates / 7g fiber

SMOKED SALMON WITH HERBED CASHEW CHEESE

MAKES 4 SERVINGS

PREP TIME: 45 MINUTES

INGREDIENTS

½ cup raw cashews

4 large cabbage leaves

2 tablespoons roughly chopped Italian flat parsley

2 tablespoons chopped chives

1 teaspoon chopped fresh tarragon

6 ounces smoked salmon, sliced

METHOD

1. Place the cashews in a heatproof bowl. Pour boiling water over them and allow to sit for 30 minutes to soften.

2. Set up a bowl of ice and water. Bring a large pot of water to a boil. Blanch the cabbage leaves for about 30 seconds, until the color is bright and they have just softened. Transfer to the ice bath.

3. Drain the cashews and transfer to a blender. Add the parsley, chives, and tarragon and puree until roughly the texture of ricotta. If the mixture seems dry, add water 1 tablespoon at a time, until it reaches this consistency.

4. Spread 2 tablespoons of cashew cheese on each cabbage leaf, add the smoked salmon, and roll into either a wrap or pinwheel shape.

PER SERVING

154 calories / 9g fat / 13g protein
5g carbohydrates / 2g fiber

HIBISCUS MUFFINS

MAKES 4 MUFFINS

A floral tea like hibiscus is perfect for muffins and other baked goods. The more I cook with tea, the more I realize how versatile it is. Once you've learned to cook with tea, you will open up a whole new world of flavor possibilities.

PREP TIME: 10 MINUTES
COOK TIME: 15 MINUTES

INGREDIENTS

¼   cup brewed hibiscus tea (brewed according to package directions)
⅔   cup almond meal/flour
1   teaspoon baking powder
    Pinch of salt
2   eggs

METHOD

1. Preheat the oven to 350°F. Coat 4 cups of a muffin tin with cooking spray.
2. In a small bowl, combine the brewed tea, almond meal, baking powder, salt, and eggs and stir with a fork to combine.
3. Spoon the batter into the muffin cups and bake until a toothpick inserted into a muffin comes out clean, 12 to 15 minutes. The muffins can be stored tightly sealed at room temperature for up to a few days.

PER MUFFIN
143 calories / 12g fat / 7g protein
4g carbohydrates / 2g fiber

CINNAMON-MULBERRY CRISP

MAKES 4 CUPS CEREAL (WITHOUT MILK)

PREP TIME: 5 MINUTES

INGREDIENTS

3   cups puffed rice cereal

¼   cup dried mulberries

1   teaspoon ground cinnamon

8   packets Monk Fruit in the Raw

4   cups unsweetened coconut milk
    beverage (such as So Delicious)

METHOD

1. In a large bowl, combine the puffed rice, mulberries, cinnamon, and monk fruit and toss well.
2. Portion into 4 bowls and add 1 cup coconut milk to each.

Tip: Add a cooked egg to your breakfast to fight hunger through to lunch.

PER SERVING
122 calories / 5g fat / 2g protein
23g carbohydrates / 2g fiber

TROPICAL OATMEAL

MAKES 4 SERVINGS

PREP TIME: 5 MINUTES
SOAK TIME: OVERNIGHT

INGREDIENTS

2   **cups rolled oats**
2   **cups unsweetened coconut milk beverage (such as So Delicious)**
¼   **cup unsweetened coconut flakes**
2   **tablespoons cacao nibs**
1½ **tablespoons diced dried mango**
4   **packets Monk Fruit in the Raw**

METHOD

In a container, combine the oats, coconut milk, coconut flakes, cacao nibs, mango, and monk fruit and mix well. Cover and refrigerate overnight. The next day, stir and serve.

PER SERVING
215 calories / 8g fat / 6g protein
33g carbohydrates / 5g fiber

VANILLA-CINNAMON-WALNUT OATMEAL

MAKES 4 SERVINGS

PREP TIME: 5 MINUTES
SOAK TIME: OVERNIGHT

INGREDIENTS

2   cups rolled oats
2   cups unsweetened coconut milk
    beverage (such as So Delicious)
1   teaspoon vanilla extract
½   teaspoon ground cinnamon
¼   cup raw walnuts
4   packets Monk Fruit in the Raw

METHOD

In a container, combine the oats, coconut milk, vanilla, cinnamon, walnuts, and monk fruit and mix well. Cover and refrigerate overnight. The next day, stir and serve.

PER SERVING
222 calories / 10g fat / 6g protein
30g carbohydrates / 5g fiber

PEANUT BUTTER–BANANA OATMEAL

MAKES 4 SERVINGS

———————

PREP TIME: 5 MINUTES
SOAK TIME: OVERNIGHT

INGREDIENTS

2   cups rolled oats

2   cups unsweetened coconut milk beverage (such as So Delicious)

4   teaspoons peanut butter powder (such as PB2)

4   packets Monk Fruit in the Raw

½   teaspoon banana extract

METHOD

In a container, combine the oats, coconut milk, peanut butter powder, monk fruit, and banana extract. Cover and refrigerate overnight. The next day, stir and serve.

PER SERVING

189 calories / 6g fat / 7g protein
30g carbohydrates / 5g fiber

SAVORY OATMEAL

MAKES 4 SERVINGS

PREP TIME: 5 MINUTES
SOAK TIME: OVERNIGHT

INGREDIENTS

1   slice turkey bacon, cooked
2   cups rolled oats
2   cups unsweetened coconut milk
    beverage (such as So Delicious)
¾   tablespoon nutritional yeast flakes
¼   cup chopped Italian flat parsley
    Salt

METHOD

In a container, combine the turkey bacon, oats, coconut milk, nutritional yeast, parsley, and salt to taste, and mix well. Cover and refrigerate overnight. The next day, stir and serve.

PER SERVING
190 calories / 6g fat / 7g protein
29g carbohydrates / 5g fiber

COCOA-RASPBERRY OATMEAL

MAKES 4 SERVINGS

PREP TIME: 5 MINUTES
SOAK TIME: OVERNIGHT

INGREDIENTS

2   cups rolled oats

2   cups unsweetened coconut milk beverage (such as So Delicious)

2   packets Monk Fruit in the Raw

1   pint raspberries

1   tablespoon stevia-sweetened chocolate chips (such as Lily's)

METHOD

In a container, combine the oats, coconut milk, monk fruit, raspberries, and chocolate chips and mix well. Cover and refrigerate overnight. The next day, stir and serve.

Tip: For more chocolate, add 1 tablespoon sugar-free chocolate sauce, or, better yet, the chocolate sauce from Key Lime Mousse (page 330).

PER SERVING
226 calories / 7g fat / 6g protein
40g carbohydrates / 10g fiber

POMEGRANATE-CHIA OVERNIGHT OATS

MAKES 4 SERVINGS

PREP TIME: 5 MINUTES
SOAK TIME: OVERNIGHT

INGREDIENTS

1   cup unsweetened coconut milk beverage (such as So Delicious)
1   cup pomegranate seeds
2   cups rolled oats
1   tablespoon chia seeds
4   packets Monk Fruit in the Raw

METHOD

1. In a blender, combine the coconut milk, pomegranate seeds, and oats and puree until smooth, about 45 seconds.
2. Remove from the blender and stir in the chia seeds and monk fruit. Refrigerate overnight.

PER SERVING
226 calories / 6g fat / 7g protein
40g carbohydrates / 8g fiber

HIGH-PROTEIN MICROWAVE ALMOND BREAD

MAKES 4 SERVINGS (2 SLICES EACH)

PREP TIME: 3 MINUTES
COOK TIME: 2 MINUTES

INGREDIENTS

⅔ cup almond meal/flour
1 teaspoon baking powder
  Pinch of salt
2 eggs
¼ cup unsweetened coconut milk beverage (such as So Delicious)

METHOD

1. Coat two large coffee mugs with cooking spray.
2. In a small bowl, mix together the almond meal, baking powder, and salt with a fork. Add the eggs and coconut milk and continue to mix with the fork.
3. Divide the mixture evenly between the mugs and microwave until a toothpick inserted in a bread comes out clean, about 90 seconds. Turn out, slice each "loaf" into 4 slices, and eat.

Tip: This bread toasts up like any other bread, either in a toaster oven or a dry skillet.

PER SERVING
143 calories / 12g fat / 7g protein
4g carbohydrates / 2g fiber

APPLE-CINNAMON BREAKFAST BARS

MAKES 4 SERVINGS

PREP TIME: 10 MINUTES

INGREDIENTS

1 cup freeze-dried apple chips

¼ cup raw pumpkin seeds

¼ cup rolled oats

2 tablespoons unsweetened sunflower seed butter (such as Once Again)

½ teaspoon ground cinnamon

1 teaspoon raw coconut nectar

METHOD

1. Place the freeze-dried apple chips in a medium bowl and crush with your hands.

2. Add the pumpkin seeds, oats, sunflower seed butter, cinnamon, and coconut nectar and mix well to combine.

3. Press into a rectangular shape and cut into 4 bars.

PER SERVING

145 calories / 8g fat / 5g protein

16g carbohydrates / 3g fiber

CRANBERRY-WALNUT BREAKFAST BARS

MAKES 4 SERVINGS

PREP TIME: 10 MINUTES

INGREDIENTS

½   cup freeze-dried cranberries

⅓   cup freeze-dried blueberries

¼   cup raw walnuts, chopped

¼   cup rolled oats

2   tablespoons unsweetened sunflower seed butter (such as Once Again)

1   tablespoon raw coconut nectar

PER SERVING

145 calories / 8g fat / 3g protein

15g carbohydrates / 3g fiber

METHOD

1. Place the freeze-dried cranberries in a medium bowl and roughly crush with your hands.
2. Add the freeze-dried blueberries, walnuts, oats, sunflower seed butter, and coconut nectar and mix well to combine.
3. Press into a rectangular shape and cut into 4 bars.

COCONUT-ALMOND BREAKFAST BARS

MAKES 4 SERVINGS

PREP TIME: 10 MINUTES

INGREDIENTS

½ cup unsweetened coconut flakes
⅓ cup whole raw almonds
1 brown rice cake, broken apart
2 tablespoons goji berries
1½ tablespoons hemp hearts
2 tablespoons unsweetened almond butter
1 tablespoon raw coconut nectar
3 packets Monk Fruit in the Raw
    Salt

METHOD

1. In a medium bowl, combine the coconut flakes, almonds, rice cake, goji berries, hemp hearts, almond butter, coconut nectar, monk fruit, and salt to taste and mix well.
2. Press into a rectangular shape and cut into 4 bars.

PER SERVING
176 calories / 11g fat / 6g protein
13g carbohydrates / 3g fiber

STRAWBERRY-PISTACHIO BREAKFAST BARS

MAKES 4 SERVINGS

PREP TIME: 10 MINUTES

INGREDIENTS

1½ cups freeze-dried strawberries

½ cup rolled oats

¼ cup raw pistachios

1   tablespoon raw coconut nectar

2   tablespoons unsweetened sunflower
    seed butter (such as Once Again)

METHOD

1. Place the strawberries in a medium bowl and roughly crush them with your hands.
2. Add the oats, pistachios, coconut nectar, and sunflower seed butter and mix well to combine.
3. Form into 4 bar shapes.

PER SERVING

169 calories / 8g fat / 5g protein
22g carbohydrates / 4g fiber

RASPBERRY-NUT BREAKFAST BARS

MAKES 4 SERVINGS

PREP TIME: 10 MINUTES

INGREDIENTS

1   cup freeze-dried raspberries
¼   cup raw cashews
1½ tablespoons flaxseeds
¼   cup rolled oats
2   tablespoons unsweetened almond butter
1½ tablespoons hemp hearts
1   tablespoon raw coconut nectar

METHOD

1. Place the freeze-dried raspberries in a medium bowl and crush with your hands.
2. Add the cashews, flaxseeds, oats, almond butter, hemp hearts, and coconut nectar and mix well to combine.
3. Press into a rectangular shape and cut into 4 bars.

PER SERVING
206 calories / 11g fat / 7g protein
19g carbohydrates / 7g fiber

PROTEIN CEREAL BARS

MAKES 4 SERVINGS

PREP TIME: 10 MINUTES

INGREDIENTS

½ cup unsweetened O-shaped cereal
   (such as Barbara's Honest O's)
1 scoop protein powder
   (such as Rocco's Protein Powder Plus)
2 tablespoons unsweetened almond butter
1 teaspoon coconut oil
Up to 4 tablespoons water

METHOD

1. Place half the cereal in a zip-top bag
   and use a rolling pin or mallet to break it
   apart. Transfer to a medium bowl.

2. Add the remaining cereal, the protein powder, almond butter, and coconut oil and stir to combine. Add the water 1 tablespoon at a time to help the mixture form a solid mass. (You may not need all of the water.)
3. Form into 4 bars and refrigerate.

PER SERVING
124 calories / 5g fat / 8g protein
9g carbohydrates / 3g fiber

PROTEIN ALMOND BUTTER BALLS

MAKES 4 SERVINGS

PREP TIME: 10 MINUTES

INGREDIENTS

5   dried apricots
1   scoop protein powder (such as Rocco's Protein Powder Plus)
¼   cup unsweetened almond butter

METHOD

1. In a food processor, combine the apricots, protein powder, and almond butter and pulse until the mixture is homogenous and a tight ball forms, about 60 seconds.
2. Roll into balls and refrigerate.

Tip: These balls are great rolled in crushed almonds or dipped in chocolate.

PER SERVING
147 calories / 10g fat / 8g protein
11g carbohydrates / 4g fiber

PROTEIN COOKIES

MAKES 4 SERVINGS

PREP TIME: 5 MINUTES
COOK TIME: 15 MINUTES

INGREDIENTS

2   eggs
⅔   cup unsweetened applesauce
¼   cup unsweetened almond milk (such as Califia Farms)
½   cup almond meal/flour
1   scoop protein powder (such as Rocco's Protein Powder Plus)
2   tablespoons chia seeds
1   teaspoon ground cinnamon

METHOD

1. Preheat the oven to 350°F. Line a mini loaf pan (8½ by 4½) with parchment paper.
2. In a medium bowl, whisk together the eggs and applesauce. Whisk in the almond milk, almond meal, protein powder, chia seeds, and cinnamon until well combined.
3. Pour the batter into the loaf pan and bake until a toothpick inserted into the center comes out clean, about 15 minutes. Let cool in the pan and slice.

Tip: Mix your favorite fruits and nuts into the batter prior to baking.

PER SERVING
183 calories / 11g fat / 12g protein
14g carbohydrates / 7g fiber

CHAPTER 5

Smoothies & Drinks

BEET-RASPBERRY SMOOTHIE

MAKES 1 SERVING

PREP TIME: 5 MINUTES

INGREDIENTS

½ cup chopped raw beets

1 cup raspberries

¾ cup water

2 packets Monk Fruit in the Raw

1 scoop protein powder
(such as Rocco's Protein Powder Plus)

METHOD

In a blender, combine the beets, raspberries, water, monk fruit, and protein powder and puree until smooth, about 1 minute.

PER SERVING

191 calories / <1g fat / 22g protein
24g carbohydrates / 13g fiber

CHOCOLATE-
MACADAMIA SMOOTHIE

MAKES 1 SERVING

PREP TIME: 5 MINUTES

INGREDIENTS

1   tablespoon raw macadamia nuts
2   teaspoons unsweetened cocoa powder
1   cup water
⅓   cup protein powder
    (such as Rocco's Protein Powder Plus)
½   cup ice
2   packets Monk Fruit in the Raw

METHOD

In a blender, combine the macadamia nuts,
cocoa, water, protein powder, ice, and monk
fruit and puree until smooth, about
1 minute.

PER SERVING
207 calories / 9g fat / 21g protein
11g carbohydrates / 10g fiber

STRAWBERRY-STARFRUIT SMOOTHIE

MAKES 1 SERVING

PREP TIME: 5 MINUTES

INGREDIENTS

½ cup water

½ cup whole frozen strawberries

1 starfruit, cut into chunks

1 scoop protein powder
   (such as Rocco's Protein Powder Plus)

2 packets Stevia in the Raw

½ cup ice

METHOD

In a blender, combine the water, strawberries, starfruit, protein powder, stevia, and ice and puree until smooth and creamy, about 1 minute.

PER SERVING

165 calories / 0g fat / 21g protein
19g carbohydrates / 13g fiber

CILANTRO-GINGER SMOOTHIE

MAKES 1 SERVING

PREP TIME: 5 MINUTES

INGREDIENTS

1   cup packed spinach

2   tablespoons chopped fresh ginger

¼   cup chopped cilantro

1   cup unsweetened coconut milk beverage
    (such as So Delicious)

2   packets Monk Fruit in the Raw

1   scoop protein powder
    (such as Rocco's Protein Powder Plus)

1   cup ice

METHOD

In a blender, combine the spinach, ginger,
cilantro, coconut milk, monk fruit, protein
powder, and ice and puree until smooth,
about 1 minute.

PER SERVING
192 calories / 5g fat / 22g protein
15g carbohydrates / 11g fiber

CUCUMBER MINT BASIL SMOOTHIE

MAKES 1 SERVING

PREP TIME: 5 MINUTES

INGREDIENTS

1   cup unsweetened coconut milk beverage
    (such as So Delicious)
1   cup sliced cucumber
½   cup spinach
20 mint leaves
10 basil leaves
2   packets Monk Fruit in the Raw
1   scoop protein powder
    (such as Rocco's Protein Powder Plus)

METHOD

In a blender, combine the coconut milk, cucumber, spinach, mint, basil, monk fruit, and protein powder and puree until smooth, about 1 minute.

PER SERVING

174 calories / 2g fat / 22g protein
16g carbohydrates / 10g fiber

PEAR-SPINACH SMOOTHIE

MAKES 1 SERVING

PREP TIME: 5 MINUTES

INGREDIENTS

½   cup spinach

½   cup chopped pear

1   cup water

½   cup ice

1   packet Monk Fruit in the Raw

1   scoop protein powder
    (such as Rocco's Protein Powder Plus)

METHOD

In a blender, combine the spinach, pear, water, ice, monk fruit, and protein powder and puree until smooth, about 1 minute.

PER SERVING

168 calories / 0g fat / 21g protein

21g carbohydrates / 11g fiber

STRAWBERRY-POMEGRANATE GREEN SMOOTHIE

MAKES 1 SERVING

PREP TIME: 5 MINUTES

INGREDIENTS

¼ cup pomegranate seeds
½ cup whole frozen strawberries
1 cup packed baby spinach
1 cup water
1 scoop protein powder
   (such as Rocco's Protein Powder Plus)

METHOD

In a blender, combine the pomegranate seeds, strawberries, spinach, water, and protein powder and puree until smooth, about 1 minute.

PER SERVING
192 calories / <1g fat / 23g protein
25g carbohydrates / 13g fiber

SEA GREEN SMOOTHIE

PREP TIME: 5 MINUTES

INGREDIENTS

½   cup unsweetened coconut milk beverage
    (such as So Delicious)
¾   cup chopped cucumber
1   teaspoon spirulina powder
½   Granny Smith apple, chopped
1   cup packed baby spinach
1   scoop protein powder
    (such as Rocco's Protein Powder Plus)
1   cup ice

METHOD

In a blender, combine the coconut milk,
cucumber, spirulina, apple, spinach, protein
powder, and ice and puree until smooth,
about 1 minute.

PER SERVING
222 calories / 3g fat / 25g protein
25g carbohydrates / 12g fiber

MOJITO SMOOTHIE

MAKES 1 SERVING

PREP TIME: 5 MINUTES

INGREDIENTS

12   mint leaves
    Juice of 1 lime
1   cup ice
½   cup unsweetened coconut milk beverage
    (such as So Delicious)
1   scoop protein powder
    (such as Rocco's Protein Powder Plus)
2   packets Monk Fruit in the Raw

METHOD

In a blender, combine the mint, lime juice,
ice, coconut milk, protein powder, and
monk fruit and puree until smooth, about
1 minute.

PER SERVING
152 calories / 2g fat / 20g protein
13g carbohydrates / 9g fiber

PEA GREEN SMOOTHIE

MAKES 1 SERVING

PREP TIME: 5 MINUTES

INGREDIENTS

⅓ cup frozen peas

½ cup spinach

1   cup water

½ cup ice

1   packet Monk Fruit in the Raw

1   scoop protein powder
    (such as Rocco's Protein Powder Plus)

METHOD

In a blender, combine the peas, spinach, water, ice, monk fruit, and protein powder and puree until smooth, about 1 minute.

PER SERVING

157 calories / 0g fat / 23g protein
15g carbohydrates / 11g fiber

CHOCOLATE-RASPBERRY SMOOTHIE

MAKES 1 SERVING

——————————————

PREP TIME: 5 MINUTES

INGREDIENTS

½ cup unsweetened coconut milk
    beverage (such as So Delicious)
½ cup raspberries
1 cup ice
1 scoop protein powder
    (such as Rocco's Protein Powder Plus)
3 packets Stevia in the Raw
1 tablespoon unsweetened cocoa powder

METHOD

In a blender, combine the coconut milk,
raspberries, ice, protein powder, stevia,
and cocoa and puree until smooth, about
1 minute.

PER SERVING

186 calories / 3g fat / 21g protein
20g carbohydrates / 13g fiber

CASHEW-MANGO SMOOTHIE

MAKES 1 SERVING

PREP TIME: 5 MINUTES

INGREDIENTS

2   tablespoons raw cashews
½   cup frozen mango
1   cup water
1   packet Monk Fruit in the Raw
1   scoop protein powder
     (such as Rocco's Protein Powder Plus)
½   cup ice

METHOD

In a blender, combine the cashews, mango, water, monk fruit, protein powder, and ice and puree until smooth, about 1 minute.

PER SERVING
252 calories / 7g fat / 23g protein
22g carbohydrates / 11g fiber

SNICKERDOODLE GREEN SMOOTHIE

MAKES 1 SERVING

PREP TIME: 5 MINUTES

INGREDIENTS

1   cup packed baby spinach

1   cup unsweetened coconut milk beverage
    (such as So Delicious)

1   scoop protein powder
    (such as Rocco's Protein Powder Plus)

½   teaspoon ground cinnamon

½   teaspoon vanilla extract

1   cup ice

METHOD

In a blender, combine the spinach, coconut milk, protein powder, cinnamon, vanilla, and ice and puree until smooth, about 1 minute.

PER SERVING

190 calories / 5g fat / 22g protein
14g carbohydrates / 12g fiber

CHOCOLATE-MINT
PROTEIN SMOOTHIE
MAKES 1 SERVING

PREP TIME: 5 MINUTES

INGREDIENTS

1   cup unsweetened coconut milk beverage
    (such as So Delicious)
½   cup ice
2   teaspoons unsweetened cocoa powder
1   scoop protein powder
    (such as Rocco's Protein Powder Plus)
2   packets Monk Fruit in the Raw
20 mint leaves

METHOD

In a blender, combine the coconut milk, ice,
cocoa, protein powder, monk fruit, and mint
and puree until smooth, about 1 minute.

PER SERVING
170 calories / 5g fat / 20g protein
12g carbohydrates / 10g fiber

SPICY MANGO MARGARITA SMOOTHIE

MAKES 1 SERVING

PREP TIME: 5 MINUTES

INGREDIENTS

½   cup water
1   scoop protein powder
    (such as Rocco's Protein Powder Plus)
¼   cup frozen mango
½   cup ice
    Juice of 1½ limes
3   packets Monk Fruit in the Raw
    Dash of hot sauce

METHOD

In a blender, combine the water, protein powder, mango, ice, lime juice, monk fruit, and hot sauce and puree until smooth, about 1 minute.

PER SERVING
165 calories / 0g fat / 20g protein
22g carbohydrates / 9g fiber

POMEGRANATE-KALE SMOOTHIE

MAKES 1 SERVING

PREP TIME: 5 MINUTES

INGREDIENTS

1   cup packed kale

½   cup unsweetened pomegranate juice

½   cup ice

2   packets Monk Fruit in the Raw

1   scoop protein powder
    (such as Rocco's Protein Powder Plus)

METHOD

In a blender, combine the kale, pomegranate juice, ice, monk fruit, and protein powder and puree until smooth, about 1 minute.

PER SERVING

223 calories / <1g fat / 32g protein

32g carbohydrates / 8g fiber

PEACH-MANGO SMOOTHIE

MAKES 1 SERVING

PREP TIME: 5 MINUTES

INGREDIENTS

½   cup water

½   cup ice

1   scoop protein powder
    (such as Rocco's Protein Powder Plus)

½   cup frozen peaches

¼   cup frozen mango

⅛   teaspoon salt

2   packets Monk Fruit in the Raw

METHOD

In a blender, combine the water, ice, protein powder, peaches, mango, salt, and monk fruit and puree until smooth, about 45 seconds.

PER SERVING

181 calories / 0g fat / 21g protein

17g carbohydrates / 10g fiber

WATERMELON CHIA REFRESHER

MAKES 1 SERVING

PREP TIME: 5 MINUTES
SOAK TIME: 10 MINUTES

INGREDIENTS

½ cup watermelon

½ cup water

3 packets Stevia in the Raw

2 tablespoons chia seeds

METHOD

In a blender, combine the watermelon, water, and stevia and puree on high until smooth, about 45 seconds. Add the chia seeds and slowly blend to combine. Let sit for at least 10 minutes. For optimum hydration, refrigerate overnight.

PER SERVING

143 calories / 9g fat / 7g protein
16g carbohydrates / 10g fiber

CRANAPPLE CHIA DRINK

MAKES 1 SERVING

PREP TIME: 5 MINUTES
SOAK TIME: 10 MINUTES

INGREDIENTS

1½ cups chopped Pink Lady apple
½   cup frozen cranberries
1   cup water
3   packets Monk Fruit in the Raw
2   tablespoons chia seeds

METHOD

In a blender, combine the apple, cranberries, water, monk fruit, and chia seeds and puree on high until smooth, about 1 minute. Let sit for at least 10 minutes. For optimum hydration, refrigerate overnight.

PER SERVING
161 calories / 5g fat/ 3g protein
31g carbohydrates / 11g fiber

PEACH AND GINGER CHIA DRINK

MAKES 1 SERVING

PREP TIME: 5 MINUTES
SOAK TIME: 10 MINUTES

INGREDIENTS

1   peach, chopped
½   cup unsweetened coconut
    milk beverage (such as So Delicious)
1   tablespoon fresh ginger
½   cup water
2   tablespoons chia seeds

METHOD

1. In a blender, combine the peach, coconut milk, ginger, and water and puree on high until smooth, about 1 minute.
2. Remove from the blender and stir in the chia seeds. Let sit for at least 10 minutes. For optimum hydration, refrigerate overnight.

PER SERVING
166 calories / 7g fat / 5g protein
27g carbohydrates / 9g fiber

SPIRULINA GREEN CHIA DRINK

MAKES 4 SERVINGS

PREP TIME: 5 MINUTES
SOAK TIME: OVERNIGHT

INGREDIENTS

1   cup unsweetened coconut
    milk beverage (such as So Delicious)
1   cup water
1   teaspoon spirulina powder
2   tablespoons chia seeds
1   cup spinach
2   packets Monk Fruit in the Raw

METHOD

1. In a bowl, stir together the coconut milk, water, spirulina powder, and chia seeds and soak for 10 minutes or up to overnight.
2. The next day, transfer the mixture to a blender. Add the spinach and monk fruit and puree until smooth.

PER SERVING
194 calories / 13g fat / 9g protein
13g carbohydrates / 11g fiber

STRAWBERRY-HIBISCUS CHIA DRINK

MAKES 1 SERVING

PREP TIME: 10 MINUTES
SOAK TIME: 10 MINUTES

INGREDIENTS

1   cup brewed hibiscus tea
    (your favorite brand)
1   cup frozen strawberries
2   packets Monk Fruit in the Raw
2   tablespoons chia seeds

METHOD

1. In a blender, combine the
   hibiscus tea, strawberries,
   and monk fruit and puree
   until smooth, about 1 minute.
2. Remove from the blender and
   stir in the chia seeds. Let sit for
   at least 10 minutes. For optimum
   hydration, refrigerate overnight.

PER SERVING
198 calories / 6g fat / 4g protein
32g carbohydrates / 9g fiber

BEET, RED PEPPER, AND APPLE JUICE

MAKES 1 SERVING

PREP TIME: 10 MINUTES
SOAK TIME: 10 MINUTES

INGREDIENTS

1   small red apple, chopped
½   medium red bell pepper, chopped
1   small red beet, peeled and chopped
1   cup water
2   packets Monk Fruit in the Raw
1   tablespoon chia seeds

METHOD

1. In a blender, combine the apple, bell pepper, beet, water, and monk fruit and puree on high until smooth, about 1 minute.
2. Remove from the blender and stir in the chia seeds. Let sit for at least 10 minutes. For optimum hydration, refrigerate overnight.

Tip: Keep already hydrated chia seeds in your refrigerator so they will be ready to go when you want them.

PER SERVING
129 calories / 5g fat / 4g protein
22g carbohydrates / 9g fiber

BERRY LEMONADE CHIA DRINK

MAKES 1 SERVING

PREP TIME: 5 MINUTES
SOAK TIME: 10 MINUTES

INGREDIENTS

1   cup raspberries
2   tablespoons lemon juice
1½ cups water
4   packets Monk Fruit in the Raw
1   tablespoon chia seeds

METHOD

1. In a blender, combine the raspberries, lemon juice, water, and monk fruit and puree until smooth, about 1 minute.
2. Remove from the blender and stir in the chia seeds. Let sit for at least 10 minutes. For optimum hydration, refrigerate overnight.

PER SERVING
142 calories / 5g fat / 5g protein
25g carbohydrates / 14g fiber

AVOCADO-CUCUMBER SMOOTHIE

MAKES 1 SERVING

PREP TIME: 5 MINUTES

INGREDIENTS

½ avocado
1 cup diced cucumber
1 cup water
2½ tablespoons lime juice
   Pinch of salt
1 packet Monk Fruit in the Raw

METHOD

In a blender, combine the avocado, cucumber, water, lime juice, salt, and monk fruit and puree until smooth, about 1 minute.

PER SERVING
137 calories / 10g fat / 3g protein
15g carbohydrates / 5g fiber

CHAPTER 6

Soups & Salads

COLD CARROT AND CURRY SOUP

MAKES 4 SERVINGS

───────────────

If, like me, you're a "souper" fan of soups, you'll love this creamy, sweet soup. The flavor of curry powder gives it a great zing. Cold soups like this one come together quickly and make for a great first course or even quick lunch in the summer.

PREP TIME: 10 MINUTES

INGREDIENTS

2   medium carrots, chopped
1   cup unsweetened coconut milk beverage (such as So Delicious)
1   teaspoon curry powder
1   tablespoon lemon juice
1   cup unsweetened nondairy coconut yogurt (such as So Delicious)
1-inch piece fresh ginger, peeled and chopped

METHOD

In a blender, combine the carrots, coconut milk, curry powder, lemon juice, yogurt, and ginger and puree until smooth, about 90 seconds.

PER SERVING

68 calories / 3g fat / <1g protein
10g carbohydrates /3g fiber

CREAM OF MUSHROOM SOUP

MAKES 4 SERVINGS

The "cream" in this cream of mushroom soup comes from almonds, which I have found to be the perfect food for creating dairy-free dishes. In fact, I think pureed almonds, prepared according to the method below, taste superior to heavy, fattening cream any day.

PREP TIME: 10 MINUTES
SOAK TIME: OVERNIGHT

INGREDIENTS

½   cup raw almonds

1   cup dried porcini mushrooms

2   cups water

1   clove garlic

6   ounces cremini mushrooms, diced
    Salt and pepper

¼   cup thyme leaves, chopped

METHOD

1. Place the almonds in a small container and add enough water to just cover. Place the dried porcini mushrooms in another small container and add the 2 cups water. Transfer both containers to the refrigerator to soak overnight.

2. Drain the almonds and transfer to a blender. Add the reconstituted porcini mushrooms, the mushroom soaking liquid, the garlic, and salt and pepper to taste. Puree on high until smooth and creamy, about 1 minute.

3. Divide among serving bowls. Top with the cremini mushrooms and thyme and serve.

PER SERVING
100 calories / 7.5g fat / 5g protein
6g carbohydrates / 2.5g fiber

RAW CURRY RAGOUT WITH DICED ZUCCHINI

MAKES 4 SERVINGS

Curried zucchini is a popular, traditional Indian dish. My rendition uses cauliflower rice to lighten the calories and carbs—and it's a raw dish, making it very filling and nutritious.

PREP TIME: 5 MINUTES
COOK TIME: 15 MINUTES

INGREDIENTS

1   head cauliflower
1   tablespoon extra-virgin olive oil
2   teaspoons curry powder
½   cup unsweetened coconut milk beverage (such as So Delicious)
    Salt and pepper
1   large zucchini, diced

METHOD

1. Shave the cauliflower on the large holes of a box grater to make "rice." Transfer to a large bowl and combine with the olive oil, curry powder, and coconut milk. Season with salt and pepper.
2. Transfer to a serving dish and top with the diced zucchini.

PER SERVING
94 calories / 5g fat / 4g protein
3g carbohydrates / 5g fiber

CAULIFLOWER SOUP

This soup is as creamy and satisfying as potato soup, without all the calories and carbs. Another plus: You don't have to cook it. It blends up in just minutes.

PREP TIME: 10 MINUTES

INGREDIENTS

1   head cauliflower, cut into florets
1   cup unsweetened coconut milk beverage (such as So Delicious)
1   cup unsweetened nondairy coconut yogurt (such as So Delicious)
2   tablespoons tahini

METHOD

In a blender, combine all the ingredients and puree until smooth, 60 to 90 seconds.

PER SERVING
118 calories / 7g fat / 4g protein
11g carbohydrates / 5g fiber

AVOCADO-CUCUMBER SOUP

MAKES 4 SERVINGS

PREP TIME: 10 MINUTES

INGREDIENTS

2   medium cucumbers, chopped

2   avocados

3   tablespoons lime juice

2   cups unsweetened coconut milk
    beverage (such as So Delicious)

½   cup cilantro

METHOD

Place the cucumbers in a blender and puree for about 30 seconds, until most of their liquid is released. Add the avocados, lime juice, coconut milk, and cilantro and puree until smooth, about 1 minute.

PER SERVING

148 calories / 12g fat / 2g protein
12g carbohydrates / 6g fiber

AJO BLANCO

MAKES 4 SERVINGS

Ajo blanco is sometimes referred to as "white gazpacho." The traditional version is made with bread, but I've omitted the carbs and gluten and added coconut yogurt to thicken this delicious soup.

PREP TIME: 10 MINUTES

INGREDIENTS

½   cup Marcona almonds
1½ cups unsweetened almond milk (such as Califia Farms)
2   tablespoons sherry vinegar
½   cup unsweetened nondairy coconut yogurt (such as So Delicious)
3   tablespoons extra-virgin olive oil
8   red grapes, halved

METHOD

1. In a blender, combine the almonds, almond milk, vinegar, and yogurt. Puree until smooth, about 1 minute.
2. With the blender running, drizzle in the olive oil. Transfer to serving bowls.
3. Garnish the soup with the halved grapes.

PER SERVING
209 calories / 20g fat / 4g protein
7g carbohydrates / 2.5g fiber

PESTO WHITE BEAN SOUP

MAKES 4 SERVINGS

PREP TIME: 15 MINUTES
COOK TIME: 20 MINUTES

INGREDIENTS

1 tablespoon extra-virgin olive oil

2 cups diced onions

2 cups sliced leeks (cut into half-moons)

1 can (15 ounces) cannellini beans, drained and rinsed

4 cups vegetable stock

1 cup basil, torn into bite-size pieces

METHOD

1. Heat the olive oil in a large pot over medium heat. Add the onions and leeks and sweat until soft and translucent, about 10 minutes.

2. Add the cannellini beans and vegetable stock and bring to a boil. Cook until the beans begin to break apart and the soup starts to thicken, about 5 minutes.

3. Remove from the heat, stir in the basil, and serve.

PER SERVING
148 calories / 4g fat / 4g protein
23g carbohydrates / 4g fiber

BEEF AND RED LENTIL SOUP

MAKES 4 SERVINGS

PREP TIME: 15 MINUTES
COOK TIME: 30 MINUTES

INGREDIENTS

1 tablespoon extra-virgin olive oil

½ cup diced celery

1 cup chopped onions

2 cups diced carrots

1 pound lean ground beef

6 cups reduced-sodium beef broth

½ cup red lentils

Salt and pepper

METHOD

1. Heat the olive oil in a large pot over medium heat. Add the onions, celery and carrots and sweat until the vegetables are tender and the onions are translucent, about 10 minutes.

2. Increase the heat to high and add the ground beef. Cook until browned, about 5 minutes, breaking up the meat with a spoon while you stir.

3. Add the beef broth and red lentils and cook until the lentils are tender and the soup thickens, 10 to 15 minutes. Season with salt and pepper.

PER SERVING

362 calories / 12g fat / 37g protein
26g carbohydrates / 6g fiber

WHITE BEAN AND BOK CHOY SOUP

MAKES 4 SERVINGS

––––––––––––––––

PREP TIME: 5 MINUTES
COOK TIME: 20 MINUTES

INGREDIENTS

1   tablespoon extra-virgin olive oil
2   cups diced onions
1   cup diced carrots
4   cups chopped bok choy
1   can (28 ounces) diced tomatoes
1   can (15 ounces) cannellini beans,
    drained and rinsed
4   cups vegetable stock
    Salt and pepper

METHOD

1. Heat the olive oil in a large pot over medium heat. Add the onions and carrots and sweat until soft and the onions are translucent, about 10 minutes.
2. Add the bok choy and tomatoes and cook until the tomatoes begin to break down, about 5 minutes.
3. Add the cannellini beans and vegetable stock and cook until the beans begin to break down and thicken the soup, 5 to 10 minutes. Season with salt and pepper.

PER SERVING
224 calories / 4g fat / 8g protein
38g carbohydrates / 10g fiber

VEGGIE CHILI

MAKES 4 SERVINGS

PREP TIME: 10 MINUTES
COOK TIME: 30 MINUTES

INGREDIENTS

1   tablespoon extra-virgin olive oil

2   cups diced onions

½   cup diced red bell pepper

2   cloves garlic, finely chopped

2   teaspoons chili powder

4   cups chopped tomatoes

1   can (15 ounces) red kidney beans, drained and rinsed

METHOD

1. Heat the olive oil in a large pot over medium heat. Add the onions and bell pepper and sweat until soft and translucent, about 10 minutes. Add the garlic and cook until soft, another 2 to 3 minutes.

2. Add the chili powder and cook for 1 minute, or until fragrant. Add the tomatoes and kidney beans and cook until thickened, about 15 minutes.

Tip: The chili gets better if you let it rest in the refrigerator overnight, so cook it a day ahead if you have the time.

PER SERVING
145 calories / 4g fat / 5g protein
23g carbohydrates / 6g fiber

COCONUT-CILANTRO CHICKEN SOUP

MAKES 4 SERVINGS

Chicken soup might have a reputation for helping us beat the winter sniffles, but that doesn't make it health food. Processed varieties, for example, can be loaded with calories, fat, and preservatives. And that doesn't take into account the lack of flavor and hunks of tough chicken. In this recipe, I sidestep all those liabilities. Plus, I make it creamy with the addition of coconut milk and fresh veggies.

PREP TIME: 10 MINUTES
COOK TIME: 20 MINUTES

INGREDIENTS

1 tablespoon coconut oil

2 cups diced onion

1½ cups diced celery

1 pound boneless, skinless chicken breast, cut into bite-size chunks

1½ cups lite coconut milk

4 cups chicken stock

Zest of 2 limes, finely grated

Salt and pepper

1½ cups cilantro leaves

METHOD

1. Heat the oil in large pot over medium heat. Add the onion and celery and sweat until soft and translucent, about 10 minutes.
2. Increase the heat to high, add the chicken, and cook until browned on all sides, about 5 minutes.
3. Add the coconut milk, chicken stock, and lime zest and bring to a boil. Cook until the chicken is tender and cooked through, about 10 minutes.
4. Season with salt and pepper and serve garnished with the cilantro.

PER SERVING
275 calories / 12g fat / 28g protein
10g carbohydrates / 2g fiber

CHICKEN CHORIZO SOUP

MAKES 4 SERVINGS

———

PREP TIME: 10 MINUTES
COOK TIME: 15 MINUTES

INGREDIENTS

1   tablespoon extra-virgin olive oil
1   cup diced onions
½   cup diced red bell pepper
1   teaspoon ancho chile powder
½   teaspoon ground cumin
2   links fully cooked chicken chorizo
    (such as Brooklyn Cured), cut into
    ½-inch-thick half-moons
4   cups reduced-sodium chicken stock
1   can (15 ounces) black beans, drained
    and rinsed
    Salt and pepper
½   cup cilantro leaves

METHOD

1. Heat the olive oil in a large pot over medium heat. Add the onions and bell pepper and sweat until soft and translucent, about 10 minutes.
2. Add the ancho powder and cumin and continue cooking for 1 to 2 minutes, until fragrant.
3. Add the chorizo, chicken stock, and black beans and bring to a boil. Cook until the beans begin to break down and thicken the soup, about 5 minutes. Season with salt and pepper. Transfer to bowls and top with the cilantro.

PER SERVING
166 calories / 7g fat / 17g protein
14g carbohydrates / 4g fiber

MANGO RADISH SALAD

Here's a salad where the sharp flavor of radish tangos with the sweetness of mango. Both flavors push and pull with each other, so expect a tasty dance in your mouth. It's dressed lightly with olive oil and lemon juice, which is my go-to dressing for most salads.

PREP TIME: 5 MINUTES

INGREDIENTS

3 cups shaved radishes

2 cups diced mango

1 cup shaved cucumber

1½ tablespoons lemon juice

1 tablespoon extra-virgin olive oil

   Salt and pepper

METHOD

In a large bowl, combine the radishes, mango, cucumber, lemon juice, olive oil, and salt and pepper to taste and toss well.

PER SERVING

89 calories / 4g fat / 1g protein

15g carbohydrates / 3g fiber

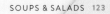

CHOPPED SALAD WITH AVOCADO CREMA DRESSING

MAKES 4 SERVINGS

———————————

PREP TIME: 20 MINUTES

INGREDIENTS

5   cups chopped napa cabbage

2½ cups chopped jicama

1   large cucumber, chopped

½   cup chopped cilantro

1   avocado

½   cup unsweetened nondairy coconut yogurt (such as So Delicious)

2   tablespoons lime juice

1   cup cherry tomatoes, halved

METHOD

1. In a large bowl, combine the napa cabbage, jicama, cucumber, and cilantro. Set aside.
2. Mash the avocado with a fork until mostly smooth. Switch to a whisk and add the yogurt and lime juice.
3. Dress the cabbage mixture and transfer to serving bowls. Top with the cherry tomatoes.

PER SERVING
132 calories / 6g fat / 3g protein
19g carbohydrates / 11g fiber

RADICCHIO CITRUS SALAD

MAKES 4 SERVINGS

Lately, I've developed a passion for radicchio, a member of the chicory family. Its slightly bitter taste adds depth to salads and pairs well with fruit, such as grapefruit, and nuts. I've used pistachios here for their sweet flavor.

PREP TIME: 10 MINUTES

INGREDIENTS

10 cups chopped radicchio
1   cup grapefruit segments, juice reserved
¼   cup raw pistachios
1   cup chopped Italian flat parsley
1   tablespoon extra-virgin olive oil
2   tablespoons grapefruit juice

METHOD

1. In a large bowl, combine the radicchio, grapefruit segments, pistachios, and parsley.
2. In a small bowl, mix the olive oil and grapefruit juice together. Pour over the salad and toss to coat.

PER SERVING
122 calories / 7g fat / 4g protein
13g carbohydrates / 2.5g fiber

STRING BEAN SALAD

MAKES 4 SERVINGS

With a grandmother who never passed a summer without a huge garden of fresh vegetables and a mother who thought it was no big deal to make pasta from scratch for nightly dinners, I was destined to value the quality of homegrown ingredients and homemade meals. I try to keep meals light, and a string bean salad made with farmers' market beans fills the bill.

PREP TIME: 15 MINUTES
COOK TIME: 7 MINUTES

INGREDIENTS

Salt

1   pound string beans, trimmed
2   cups cherry tomatoes, halved
½   cup chopped chives
2   tablespoons red wine vinegar
1   tablespoon extra-virgin olive oil

METHOD

1. Bring a large pot of water to a boil.
2. Add some salt to the water and boil the beans until tender, about 7 minutes. Drain the beans and let cool.
3. In a large bowl, combine the beans, tomatoes, chives, vinegar, and olive oil. Season with salt and toss well to coat.

PER SERVING

79 calories / 4g fat / 3g protein
11g carbohydrates / 5g fiber

KALE TABBOULEH

MAKES 4 SERVINGS

PREP TIME: 15 MINUTES
COOK TIME: 15 MINUTES

INGREDIENTS

- ⅔ cup cooked quinoa (cooked according to package directions)
- 5 ounces baby kale, cut into bite-size pieces
- 2 dried apricots, diced
- 2 tablespoons raw pumpkin seeds
- 1 tablespoon lemon juice
- 1 tablespoon extra-virgin olive oil

METHOD

In a large bowl, combine the cooked quinoa, kale, apricots, pumpkin seeds, lemon juice, and olive oil and mix well.

PER SERVING
109 calories / 5g fat / 12g protein
12g carbohydrates / 2g fiber

ROASTED BEET SALAD

MAKES 4 SERVINGS

I love to make my own cashew cheese. It's a delicious, satisfying alternative to my favorite dairy cheeses. Cashew cheese is loaded with protein and minerals, but contains zero cholesterol and lots of heart-healthy monounsaturated fats. In this recipe, the cheese pairs with roasted beets for a delightful salad.

PREP TIME: 20 MINUTES
SOAK TIME: 2 HOURS TO OVERNIGHT
COOK TIME: 1 HOUR 15 MINUTES

INGREDIENTS

½ cup raw cashews

¼ cup plus 2 teaspoons apple cider vinegar

½ pound beets, topped and tailed

1 tablespoon olive oil

Salt and pepper

1 tablespoon coconut oil

1 cup basil leaves

8 cups baby chard salad mix

METHOD

1. Preheat the oven to 400°F.
2. Place the cashews in a small container and add enough water to just cover. Transfer to the refrigerator to soak for at least 2 hours or up to overnight.
3. Reserving the soaking water, drain the cashews and transfer to a food processor. Add 2 teaspoons of the vinegar and pulse until it achieves the consistency of ricotta. If the mixture is dry, add some of the soaking liquid 1 tablespoon at a time until it comes together.
4. Brush the beets very lightly with olive oil and season with salt and pepper. Place on a baking sheet and roast until they offer no resistance when punctured with a paring knife, about 1 hour and 15 minutes. Allow the beets to cool.
5. In a bowl, whisk together half the cashew cheese, the remaining ¼ cup vinegar, and the coconut oil. Set the dressing aside.
6. Peel the beets and cut into bite-size wedges. Place in a small bowl. Chop ¼ cup of the basil, add it to the beets, and toss.
7. In a large bowl, combine the salad mix and the remaining basil leaves, tearing them into bite-size pieces. Add the dressing and mix.
8. Place the salad greens in a serving dish and top with the beets and the remaining cashew cheese.

Tip: To cut down on your prep time, look for pre-cooked beets in packages at the grocery store.

PER SERVING
162 calories / 4g fat / 4g protein
15g carbohydrates / 4g fiber

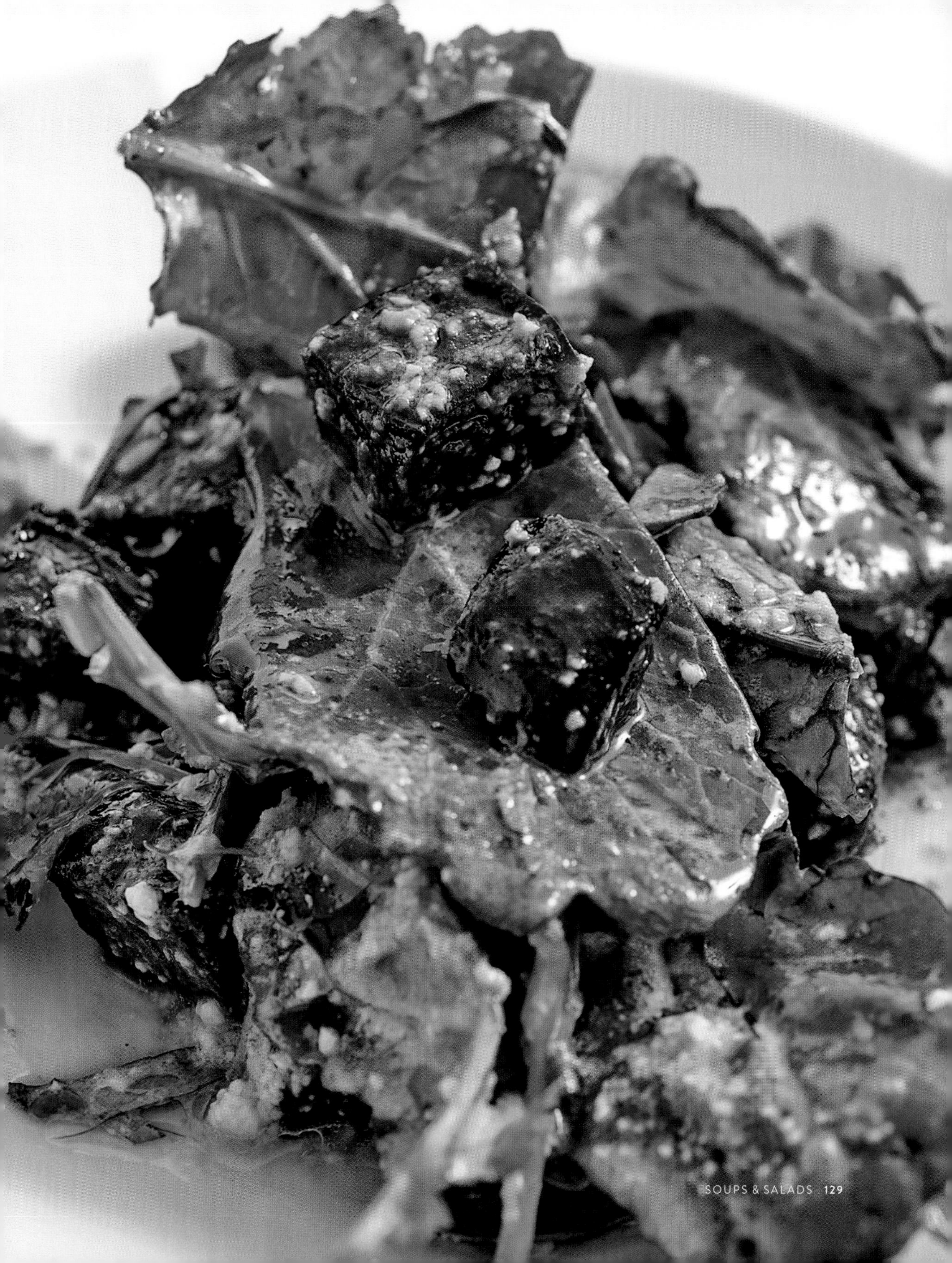

ARUGULA MELON SALAD

I love arugula. But I think it needs a special something with it. In this recipe, I've matched it with cantaloupe for a delicious low-calorie salad that will make your often-tortured bathroom scale give thanks.

PREP TIME: 15 MINUTES

INGREDIENTS

1   bag (10 ounces) arugula
2   cups cubed cantaloupe
¼   cup apple cider vinegar
1   tablespoon extra-virgin olive oil
     Salt and pepper

METHOD

In a large bowl, combine the arugula and cantaloupe. Add the vinegar, olive oil, and salt and pepper to taste and toss well to coat.

PER SERVING
78 calories / 4g fat / 2g protein
11g carbohydrates / 2g fiber

ESCAROLE, WALNUT, AND APPLE SALAD

MAKES 4 SERVINGS

———————————

Escarole is delicious and packed with nutrients, but most people don't know what to do with it, so it ends up being largely neglected. That changes with this salad! When paired with sweet apples, crunchy walnuts, and a light, creamy dressing, you are guaranteed to become an escarole fan.

PREP TIME: 15 MINUTES

INGREDIENTS

- 8 cups chopped escarole
- ½ cup raw walnuts
- 2 cups chopped Granny Smith apples
- ½ cup unsweetened nondairy coconut yogurt (such as So Delicious)
- 1 tablespoon lemon juice
- 2 packets Monk Fruit in the Raw

METHOD

1. In a large bowl, combine the escarole, walnuts, and apples.
2. In a small bowl, stir together the coconut yogurt, lemon juice, and monk fruit and mix well. Pour over the escarole, toss to coat evenly, and serve.

PER SERVING
134 calories / 9.5g fat / 3g protein
10g carbohydrates / 4g fiber

BROCCOLI FRUIT SALAD

MAKES 4 SERVINGS

When broccoli meets grapefruit, watch out:
You've got an explosion of flavor—not to
mention a huge dose of nutrition. To make the
grapefruit zest, simply grate the grapefruit
skin on a grater or Microplane. Be sure to buy
organic grapefruit, since the skin of citrus
absorbs a lot of pesticides.

PREP TIME: 15 MINUTES

INGREDIENTS

2   bags (10 ounces each) broccoli slaw mix
1   tablespoon grated grapefruit zest
2   tablespoons fresh grapefruit juice
½   cup diced grapefruit
½   cup unsweetened nondairy coconut
    yogurt (such as So Delicious)
1   tablespoon white wine vinegar

METHOD

In a large bowl, combine the slaw mix,
grapefruit zest and juice, diced grapefruit,
yogurt, and vinegar and stir well to
combine.

PER SERVING
102 calories / 1g fat / 4g protein
21g carbohydrates / 5g fiber

HEIRLOOM TOMATO SALAD

MAKES 4 SERVINGS

———

I love to cook with heirloom tomatoes. An heirloom tomato, or any heirloom vegetable for that matter, is generally considered to be a variety of seed that has been passed down through several generations because of its valued characteristics—in other words, a pedigree in the vegetable world. Not only are they delicious, heirloom tomatoes are thought to be richer in vitamin C than conventional tomatoes.

PREP TIME: 10 MINUTES

INGREDIENTS

2   pounds heirloom tomatoes, cut into bite-size wedges
2   tablespoons extra-virgin olive oil
¼   cup chopped Italian flat parsley
3   tablespoons chopped chives
3   tablespoons chopped basil
¼   cup champagne vinegar

METHOD

In a large bowl, combine the tomatoes, olive oil, parsley, chives, basil, and vinegar and toss to coat.

Tip: Add a sliced red onion for a nice crunch.

PER SERVING
108 calories / 7g fat / 2g protein
12g carbohydrates / 3g fiber

KALE, STRAWBERRY, AND BALSAMIC SALAD

MAKES 4 SERVINGS

You know you should be eating kale for its superfood status, but how in the world do you prepare it raw? After all, raw kale can be pretty bitter. I have the perfect solution with this salad. The sweetness of the strawberries cuts right through the bitterness of the kale.

PREP TIME: 10 MINUTES

INGREDIENTS

8 cups baby kale
2 tablespoons extra-virgin olive oil
3 tablespoons balsamic vinegar
2 cups sliced strawberries

METHOD

1. Place the kale in a large bowl. Add the olive oil and vinegar and mix well.
2. Divide among serving bowls and top with the strawberries.

Tip: The strawberries in this salad are very important to its flavor, so use only the freshest strawberries at the height of their season, preferably purchased from your closest farmers' market.

PER SERVING
135 calories / 8g fat / 3g protein
17g carbohydrates / 3g fiber

GREEK SALAD

MAKES 4 SERVINGS

"Salad" doesn't always mean leafy green vegetables like lettuce. Sometimes I like to create salads without any leafy greens, and my version of a Greek salad does just that. You won't miss the lettuce!

PREP TIME: 20 MINUTES
COOK TIME: 15 MINUTES

INGREDIENTS

3   cups broccoli florets

3½ cups cauliflower florets

1½ cups chopped cucumber

1   cup halved cherry tomatoes

¼   cup Kalamata olives, pitted

½   cup chopped dill

2   tablespoons chopped oregano

3   tablespoons sherry vinegar

1   tablespoon extra-virgin olive oil

METHOD

1. Set up a bowl of ice and water. Bring a large pot of water to a boil.
2. Add the broccoli florets to the boiling water and cook until tender, about 5 minutes. Transfer to the ice bath. Add the cauliflower to the boiling water and cook until tender, about 7 minutes. Remove and place in the ice bath.
3. Drain the broccoli and cauliflower and transfer to a large bowl. Add the cucumber, tomatoes, olives, dill, oregano, vinegar, and olive oil. Toss well to coat and serve.

Tip: Skip the cooking and simply chop up fresh broccoli and cauliflower if you prefer a raw salad.

PER SERVING
144 calories / 8g fat / 5g protein
17g carbohydrates / 6g fiber

HOLY GRAIL KALE SALAD

MAKES 4 SERVINGS

PREP TIME: 15 MINUTES

INGREDIENTS

1   cup blueberries
½   cup unsweetened nondairy coconut
     yogurt (such as So Delicious)
2   teaspoons lemon juice
2   packets Monk Fruit in the Raw
8   cups baby kale
½   cup raw almonds

METHOD

1. Place half of the blueberries in a medium
   bowl. Add the yogurt, lemon juice, and
   monk fruit. Use a whisk to break the
   blueberries up against the sides of the
   bowl and mix the dressing together.
2. In a large bowl, toss the kale with the
   dressing and divide equally among
   4 bowls. Top with the remaining
   blueberries and the almonds.

PER SERVING

187 calories / 10g fat / 6g protein
21g carbohydrates / 3g fiber

ASPARAGUS AND TOMATO SALAD

MAKES 4 SERVINGS

Looking for something colorful, healthful, and easy to make for Easter? Try this salad. Its lovely green and red hues announce spring. It has a great nutritional profile, too. And the cooking is minimal; you just quickly sauté asparagus and add it to the tomatoes.

PREP TIME: 10 MINUTES
COOK TIME: 5 MINUTES

INGREDIENTS

1 tablespoon extra-virgin olive oil
1 bunch pencil asparagus, cut into 2-inch pieces
   Leaves from ½ sprig rosemary
2 cups halved cherry tomatoes
1 tablespoon champagne vinegar
   Salt and pepper

METHOD

1. Heat the olive oil in a large sauté pan over high heat. When the oil just begins to smoke, add the asparagus and rosemary and cook, stirring frequently, until softened, about 5 minutes.
2. Transfer the asparagus to a large bowl and add the tomatoes and vinegar. Season with salt and pepper and serve.

PER SERVING
50 calories / 4g fat / 1g protein
4g carbohydrates / 2g fiber

SUMMER FRUIT SALAD

MAKES 4 SERVINGS

Cool off on a hot summer day with this refreshing fruit salad. It's beautiful and simple to assemble. The hazelnut oil lends a special nutty taste that pairs nicely with the fruit. Brimming with nutrition, this salad is perfect for backyard barbecues, brunches, snacking, or even dessert.

PREP TIME: 10 MINUTES

INGREDIENTS

3 plums, diced
4 apricots, diced
1 peach, diced
1 tablespoon chopped tarragon
2 tablespoons chopped mint
1 tablespoon hazelnut oil
¼ cup unsweetened nondairy coconut yogurt (such as So Delicious)

METHOD

In a large bowl, combine the plums, apricots, peach, tarragon, mint, oil, and yogurt and toss to combine.

PER SERVING
133 calories / 5g fat / 2g protein
23g carbohydrates / 4g fiber

SWEET POTATO AND OKRA SALAD

MAKES 4 SERVINGS

PREP TIME: 15 MINUTES
COOK TIME: 15 MINUTES

INGREDIENTS

2 small sweet potatoes
1 tablespoon extra-virgin olive oil
½ pound okra
2 tablespoons red wine vinegar
¼ cup chopped Italian flat parsley
   Salt and pepper

PER SERVING
151 calories / 4g fat / 3g protein
28g carbohydrates / 5g fiber

METHOD

1. Pierce the sweet potatoes in several places with a paring knife. Place on a microwave-safe dish and cook until the sweet potatoes are just cooked through, about 7 minutes. Set aside until cool enough to handle.

2. Heat the olive oil in a large sauté pan over high heat. When the oil just begins to smoke, add the okra and cook until the okra softens and the pods begin to burst, about 10 minutes.

3. Peel the sweet potatoes, cut into bite-size cubes, and place in a large bowl.

4. Cut the okra into 1-inch-thick rounds and add to the bowl as well.

5. Add the vinegar, parsley, and salt and pepper to taste and toss well to combine.

CHICKEN CAESAR SALAD

MAKES 4 SERVINGS

A great Caesar salad recipe gets its groove from a great Caesar dressing recipe. But most dressings are made with loads of mayonnaise, and therefore are high in fat and calories. My favorite swap for mayonnaise is coconut yogurt. Along with garlic, anchovies (yes, gotta have em!), lemon juice, and olive oil, the yogurt makes a delicious Caesar dressing.

PREP TIME: 10 MINUTES
COOK TIME: 15 MINUTES

INGREDIENTS

¾ pound boneless, skinless chicken breast
2 cloves garlic
3 anchovy fillets
2 tablespoons lemon juice
½ cup unsweetened nondairy coconut yogurt (such as So Delicious)
3 tablespoons extra-virgin olive oil
4 hearts romaine, chopped
¼ cup grated Parmesan cheese

METHOD

1. Preheat the oven to 350°F.
2. Place the chicken on a baking sheet and bake until the internal temperature is 165°F, 12 to 15 minutes. Remove from the oven to rest.
3. In a blender, combine the garlic, anchovies, lemon juice, and yogurt and puree. While the blender is running, drizzle in the olive oil.
4. Mix the romaine and dressing together in a bowl and divide among 4 plates. Slice the chicken and place on top of the romaine. Top everything with the grated Parmesan.

PER SERVING
228 calories / 10g fat / 23g protein
9g carbohydrates / 4g fiber

HERB LENTIL SALAD

MAKES 4 SERVINGS

PREP TIME: 10 MINUTES
COOK TIME: 15 MINUTES

INGREDIENTS

1   cup small green (Puy) lentils

2   cups diced onions

1½ cups diced carrots

1   cup diced celery

About 2 cups water

2   tablespoons white wine vinegar

¼   cup chopped dill

2   tablespoons chopped tarragon

METHOD

1. To reduce your cooking time, soak the lentils in water overnight. This step is not necessary, but time is greatly reduced if you do this.

2. Sweat the onions, carrots, and celery in a medium pot until softened, about 10 minutes. Add the lentils and water to just cover. Cover the pot and cook until the lentils are tender, 5 to 10 minutes. Drain any liquid that remains.

3. Place the lentil mixture in a large bowl. Add the vinegar, dill, and tarragon. Toss to combine.

PER SERVING
170 calories / <1g fat / 13g protein
30g carbohydrates / 7g fiber

SHRIMP SALAD WITH JUNIPER AND CUCUMBER

MAKES 4 SERVINGS

Frisée is a type of chicory that has become popular in recent years, though it's been a favorite among chefs for a while now. If you're not familiar with frisée, it looks like lettuce that has gone frizzy. You can buy it at many upscale grocers and at some farmers' markets.

PREP TIME: 15 MINUTES
COOK TIME: 5 MINUTES

INGREDIENTS

¾ pound shrimp, peeled and deveined

1 bag (10 ounces) arugula

2½ cups hand-torn frisée

½ cup chopped celery

1½ cups chopped cucumber

1 teaspoon juniper berries

2 tablespoons lemon juice

1 tablespoon extra-virgin olive oil

METHOD

1. Set up a bowl of ice and water. Bring a large pot of water to a boil. Add the shrimp to the boiling water and cook until tender, about 3 minutes. Transfer to the ice bath.

2. In a large bowl, combine the arugula, frisée, celery, and cucumber. Add the shrimp.

3. In a small bowl, crush the juniper berries with the lemon juice and olive oil. Pour over the salad greens and toss well.

PER SERVING

156 calories / 6g fat / 20g protein
8g carbohydrates / 3g fiber

SWEET POTATO SALAD WITH FLAKED SALMON

MAKES 4 SERVINGS

___

Here, I've matched sweet potatoes with salmon for a delicious low-calorie main-dish salad. Salmon is good and good for you. It's naturally tender, easy to digest, low in bad fats and cholesterol, and loaded with beneficial nutrients and oils. The salmon here is quick to bake; then all you have to do is fold it into a mixture of sweet potatoes and other delicious ingredients.

PREP TIME: 15 MINUTES
COOK TIME: 15 MINUTES

INGREDIENTS

2   medium sweet potatoes

½   pound wild-caught skinless, boneless, salmon fillet

½   cup chopped scallions

½   cup unsweetened nondairy coconut yogurt (such as So Delicious)

3   tablespoons apple cider vinegar

METHOD

1. Preheat the oven to 375°F. Line a baking sheet with parchment paper.

2. Meanwhile, pierce the skin of the sweet potatoes with a paring knife. Microwave until the potatoes are tender, 7 to 10 minutes. Set aside until cool enough to handle.

3. Bake the salmon on the lined baking sheet until the fish is tender and flakes easily, about 15 minutes.

4. Scoop the inside of the sweet potatoes into a large bowl. Add the scallions, yogurt, and vinegar and whisk to combine and break up the sweet potatoes.

5. Tear the salmon apart with your hands and gently fold it into the sweet potatoes with a large spoon.

PER SERVING
211 calories / 7g fat / 13g protein
23g carbohydrates / 4g fiber

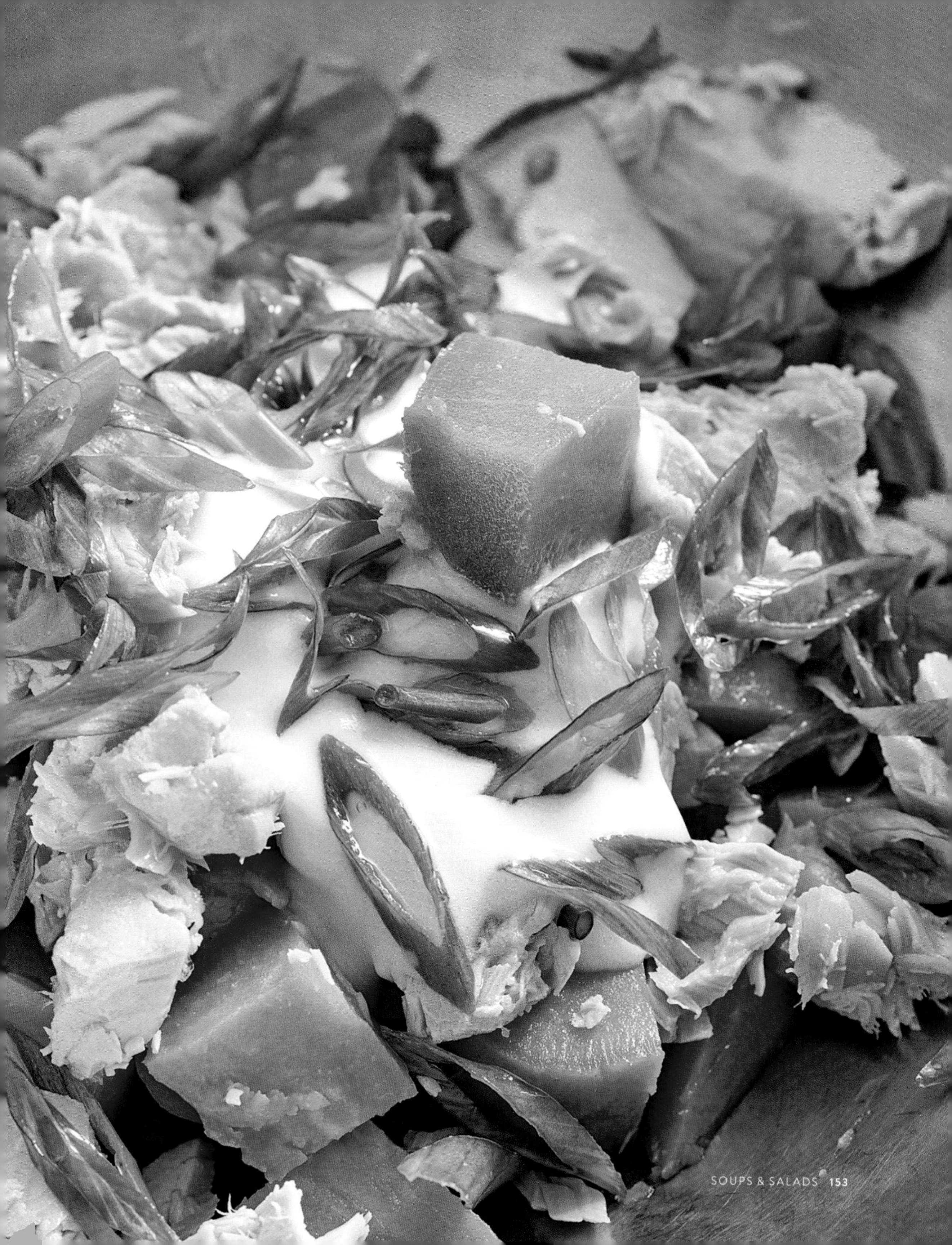

PEPPERY GREEN SALAD WITH PULLED CHICKEN AND LIME DRESSING

MAKES 4 SERVINGS

I call this salad "peppery" because mustard greens tend to be deliciously peppery in taste. Add a dressing made with sweet monk fruit and creamy coconut yogurt and you've got a chicken salad like no other.

PREP TIME: 10 MINUTES
COOK TIME: 15 MINUTES

INGREDIENTS

- ½ pound chicken thighs
- 8 ounces mustard greens salad blend (such as Organicgirl Peppergreens)
- ½ cup unsweetened nondairy coconut yogurt (such as So Delicious)
- 2 teaspoons grated lime zest
- 2 tablespoons lime juice
- 2 packets Monk Fruit in the Raw
- 1½ cups multicolor cherry tomatoes, halved

METHOD

1. In a pot, combine the chicken with water just to cover. Bring to a boil and cook until cooked through, about 15 minutes. Drain and let cool, then pull apart with your hands. Set aside.

2. Place the salad greens in a large bowl. In a smaller bowl, whisk together the coconut yogurt, lime zest, lime juice, and monk fruit. Pour over the greens and mix well to coat.

3. Divide the greens among 4 plates. Top each salad with the chicken and cherry tomatoes.

Tip: Keep cooked chicken in your refrigerator. It will always be ready to go and will dramatically cut your prep time.

PER SERVING
98 calories / 2g fat / 15g protein
5g carbohydrates / 2g fiber

CHAPTER 7

Veggie Burgers

ROCCO'S PROTEIN BUNS

Sometimes it's tough to find gluten-free bread or buns without a lot of extraneous stuff and preservatives. So why not make your own? Here is a simple recipe that doesn't even require yeast. The burger recipes on the following pages (and shown on pages 161 and 168) use these protein-power buns.

PREP TIME: 10 MINUTES
COOK TIME: 15 MINUTES

INGREDIENTS

2   scoops Rocco's Protein Baking Mix or your favorite baking mix (such as Bob's Red Mill)
¼   cup almond meal/flour
1   teaspoon baking powder
2   packets Monk Fruit in the Raw
     Pinch of salt
2   eggs
½   cup liquid egg whites

METHOD

1. Preheat the oven to 350°F. Line a baking sheet with parchment paper.
2. In a medium bowl, whisk together the protein baking mix, almond meal, baking powder, monk fruit, and salt, making sure to remove as many lumps as possible. Add the whole eggs and mix well to form a thick mass. Set aside.
3. In a medium bowl, with an electric mixer, beat the liquid egg whites until stiff peaks form. Fold this into the protein and almond mixture in three installments. Scoop this into 4 even portions onto the lined baking sheet.
4. Transfer to the oven and bake until a toothpick inserted into the center of the bun comes out clean, about 15 minutes. Remove from the oven to cool, then serve immediately.

PER BUN
144 calories / 6g fat / 18g protein
6g carbohydrates / 5g fiber

QUINOA-KALE VEGGIE BURGER

MAKES 4 SERVINGS

Here's what I call a "super burger" because it is made with three superfoods—quinoa, kale, and avocado. The flavor combination of these three catapult it into the category of super delicious, too. Make sure to really pack in the mixture tightly when making the patties, to ensure a dense and more stable burger.

PREP TIME: 10 MINUTES
COOK TIME: 15 MINUTES

INGREDIENTS

1   avocado
2   tablespoons lime juice
1   cup cooked quinoa
2   cups finely chopped kale
1   scoop Rocco's Protein Baking Mix or your favorite baking mix (such as Bob's Red Mill)
¼   cup water
4   Rocco's Protein Buns (page 158), toasted
½   tomato, sliced
¼   red onion, sliced

METHOD

1. Preheat the oven to 400°F.
2. Scoop the avocado into a large bowl and add the lime juice. Mix together with a fork, but leave a few chunks.
3. Add the quinoa, kale, protein baking mix, and water and mix to combine. Form into 4 patties.
4. Transfer to a baking sheet and bake for 10 minutes to set the proteins in the patties. Grill them afterward if you would like, or eat as is.
5. Serve on the protein buns garnished with the tomato and red onion.

PER SERVING (WITHOUT BUN)
287 calories / 12g fat / 26g protein
22g carbohydrates / 11g fiber

CHICKPEA VEGGIE BURGERS

MAKES 4 SERVINGS

PREP TIME: 15 MINUTES
COOK TIME: 15 MINUTES

INGREDIENTS

1½ cups canned chickpeas,
    drained and rinsed
½ cup chopped mint
½ cup chopped parsley
½ cup chopped cilantro
1 teaspoon ground cumin
1 scoop Rocco's Protein Baking Mix or
    your favorite baking mix (such as Bob's
    Red Mill)
¼ cup water
    Salt and pepper
4 Rocco's Protein Buns (page 158),
    toasted
½ tomato, sliced
¼ red onion, sliced

METHOD

1. Preheat the oven to 350°F.
2. Roughly chop the chickpeas and place in a large bowl with the mint, parsley, cilantro, cumin, protein baking mix, and water. Season with salt and pepper. Mix well and form into 4 patties.
3. Transfer to a baking sheet and bake for 10 minutes to set the proteins in the patties. Grill them afterward if you would like, or eat as is.
4. Serve on the protein buns garnished with the tomato and red onion.

Tip: You can use the Tzatziki (page 249) for a great burger spread.

PER SERVING (WITHOUT BUN)
244 calories / 7g fat / 27g protein
19g carbohydrates / 10g fiber

Chickpea Veggie
Burger

Thai Veggie
Burger

Quinoa-Kale
Veggie Burger

Asian Veggie
Burger

Southwest
Chili Burger

THAI VEGGIE BURGERS

MAKES 4 SERVINGS

PREP TIME: 10 MINUTES
COOK TIME: 15 MINUTES

INGREDIENTS

1½ cups canned black beans, drained and
    rinsed

½   cup raw cashews, chopped

5   ounces shiitake mushrooms, chopped
    Salt and pepper

1   scoop Rocco's Protein Baking Mix or
    your favorite baking mix (such as Bob's
    Red Mill)

¼   cup water

1   tablespoon green curry paste

4   Rocco's Protein Buns (page 158),
    toasted

½   tomato, sliced

¼   red onion, sliced

METHOD

1. Preheat the oven to 400°F and line a
   baking sheet with parchment.

2. Roughly chop the black beans and place
   in a large bowl. Add the cashews, shiitake
   mushrooms, salt and pepper to taste,
   protein baking mix, water, and green
   curry paste and mix well. Form into
   4 patties.

3. Transfer to the baking sheet and bake
   for 10 minutes to set the proteins in the
   patties. Grill them afterward if you would
   like, or eat as is.

4. Serve on the protein buns garnished with
   the tomato and red onion.

PER SERVING (WITHOUT BUN)
298 calories / 10g fat / 29g protein
23g carbohydrates / 12g fiber

SOUTHWEST CHILI BURGERS

MAKES 4 SERVINGS

PREP TIME: 15 MINUTES
COOK TIME: 15 MINUTES

INGREDIENTS

¼ cup frozen corn kernels

1½ cups canned black beans, drained and rinsed

½ cup chopped cilantro

2 teaspoons chili powder
Salt and pepper

1 scoop Rocco's Protein Baking Mix or your favorite baking mix (such as Bob's Red Mill)

¼ cup water

4 Rocco's Protein Buns (page 158), toasted

½ tomato, sliced

¼ red onion, sliced

METHOD

1. Preheat the oven to 350°F.
2. In a medium saucepan of boiling water, cook the corn until tender, about 3 minutes. Drain and transfer to a large bowl.
3. Chop the black beans and add to the corn. Then add the cilantro, chili powder, salt and pepper to taste, protein baking mix, and water and mix well. Form into 4 patties.
4. Transfer to a baking sheet and bake for 10 minutes to set the proteins in the patties. Grill them afterward if you would like, or eat as is.
5. Serve on the protein buns garnished with the tomato and red onion.

Tip: Add some spicy salsa for an extra kick.

PER SERVING (WITHOUT BUN)
251 calories / 7g fat / 27g protein
21g carbohydrates / 11g fiber

ASIAN VEGGIE BURGERS

MAKES 4 SERVINGS

PREP TIME: 15 MINUTES
COOK TIME: 15 MINUTES

INGREDIENTS

5 ounces shiitake mushrooms, stems discarded, caps sliced

2 cups canned red beans, drained and rinsed

1 tablespoon reduced-sodium tamari

1 teaspoon ground ginger

½ cup chopped cilantro
Salt and pepper

1 scoop Rocco's Protein Baking Mix or your favorite baking mix (such as Bob's Red Mill)

¼ cup water

4 Rocco's Protein Buns (page 158), toasted

½ tomato, sliced

¼ red onion, sliced

METHOD

1. Preheat the oven to 350°F.
2. Heat a large nonstick sauté pan over high heat. Add the shiitake mushrooms and cook until browned and tender, about 5 minutes. Transfer to a cutting board.
3. Roughly chop the shiitake mushrooms and red beans and place in a large bowl. Add the tamari, ginger, cilantro, salt and pepper to taste, the protein baking mix, and water and mix well. Form into 4 patties.
4. Transfer to a baking sheet and bake for 10 minutes to set the proteins in the patties. Grill them afterward if you would like, or eat as is.
5. Serve on the protein buns garnished with the tomato and red onion.

PER SERVING (WITHOUT BUN)
247 calories / 6g fat / 29g protein
21g carbohydrates / 13g fiber

ALMOND VEGGIE BURGERS

MAKES 4 SERVINGS

PREP TIME: 15 MINUTES
COOK TIME: 15 MINUTES

INGREDIENTS

1½ cups canned black beans (such as Eden Organics), drained and rinsed
¼ cup raw almonds
1   cup chopped onion
1½ tablespoons nutritional yeast
    Salt and pepper
1   scoop Rocco's Protein Baking Mix or your favorite baking mix (such as Bob's Red Mill)
½ cup water
4   Rocco's Protein Buns (page 158), toasted
½ tomato, sliced
¼ red onion, sliced

METHOD

1. Preheat the oven to 350°F.
2. Roughly chop the black beans and almonds and place in a large bowl. Add the onion, nutritional yeast, salt and pepper to taste, the protein baking mix, and water and mix well. Form into 4 patties.

3. Transfer to a baking sheet and bake for 10 minutes to set the proteins in the patties. Grill them afterward if you would like, or eat as is.
4. Serve on the protein buns garnished with the tomato and red onion.

Tip: Try putting almond butter on your bun instead of the usual ketchup.

PER SERVING (WITHOUT BUN)
305 calories / 11g fat / 30g protein
23g carbohydrates / 12g fiber

FAJITA VEGGIE BURGERS

MAKES 4 SERVINGS

PREP TIME: 15 MINUTES
COOK TIME: 15 MINUTES

INGREDIENTS

1   cup cooked quinoa (cooked according to package directions)
⅓   cup chopped green bell pepper
1   teaspoon chili powder
½   teaspoon ground cumin
1   scoop Rocco's Protein Baking Mix
¼   cup water
    Salt and pepper
5   ounces shiitake mushrooms, chopped
4   Rocco's Protein Buns (page 158), toasted
½   cup salsa (such as Brad's Organic)
¼   red onion, sliced

METHOD

1. Preheat the oven to 350°F.
2. In a large bowl, stir together the quinoa, bell pepper, chili powder, cumin, protein baking mix, water, salt and pepper to taste, and the shiitake mushrooms. Form into 4 patties.
2. Transfer to a baking sheet and bake for 10 minutes to set the proteins in the patties. Grill them afterward if you would like, or eat as is.
3. Serve on the protein buns garnished with the salsa and red onion.

PER SERVING (WITHOUT BUN)
249 calories / 7g fat / 26g protein
22g carbohydrates / 9g fiber

CAJUN VEGGIE BURGERS

MAKES 4 SERVINGS

PREP TIME: 10 MINUTES
COOK TIME: 15 MINUTES

INGREDIENTS

2 cups canned red kidney beans, drained and rinsed

¾ cup chopped celery

¼ cup chopped bell pepper

1 tablespoon Cajun seasoning
 Salt and pepper

1 scoop Rocco's Protein Baking Mix or your favorite baking mix (such as Bob's Red Mill)

4 Rocco's Protein Buns (page 158), toasted

½ tomato, sliced

¼ red onion, sliced

METHOD

1. Preheat the oven to 350°F.
2. Roughly chop the red kidney beans. Place them in a large bowl along with the celery, bell pepper, Cajun seasoning, salt and pepper to taste, and the protein baking mix and mix well. Form into 4 patties.
3. Transfer to a baking sheet and bake for 10 minutes to set the proteins in the patties. Grill them afterward if you would like, or eat as is.
4. Serve on the protein buns garnished with the tomato and red onion.

PER SERVING (WITHOUT BUN)
232 calories / 6g fat / 27g protein
19g carbohydrates / 12g fiber

KIWI VEGGIE BURGERS

MAKES 4 SERVINGS

PREP TIME: 10 MINUTES
COOK TIME: 15 MINUTES

INGREDIENTS

1½ cups canned black beans, drained and rinsed

1 cup chopped canned beets

1 cup chopped onion

1½ tablespoons nutritional yeast
 Salt and pepper

1 scoop Rocco's Protein Baking Mix or your favorite baking mix (such as Bob's Red Mill)

4 eggs

4 Rocco's Protein Buns (page 158), toasted

½ tomato, sliced

¼ red onion, sliced

METHOD

1. Preheat the oven to 350°F.
2. Roughly chop the black beans and place in a large bowl. Add the beets, onion, nutritional yeast, salt and pepper to taste, and the protein baking mix and mix well. Form into 4 patties.

3. Transfer to a baking sheet and bake for 10 minutes to set the proteins in the patties. Grill them afterward if you would like, or eat as is.
4. In a large nonstick pan, cook the eggs to sunny side up.
5. Serve the burgers on the protein buns and top each with an egg, and tomato and red onion slices.

PER SERVING (WITHOUT BUN)
348 calories / 12g fat / 35g protein
25g carbohydrates / 12g fiber

CURRY IN A HURRY BURGERS

MAKES 4 SERVINGS

PREP TIME: 10 MINUTES
COOK TIME: 20 MINUTES

INGREDIENTS

5 ounces shiitake mushrooms, sliced
¾ cup canned chickpeas, drained and rinsed
2 teaspoons curry powder
½ teaspoon ground cumin
½ cup Rocco's Protein Baking Mix or your favorite baking mix (such as Bob's Red Mill)
¼ cup water
Salt and pepper
4 Rocco's Protein Buns (page 158), toasted
½ tomato, sliced
¼ red onion, sliced
¾ cup grated carrots (grated on large holes of a box grater)

METHOD

1. Preheat the oven to 350°F.
2. Heat a large nonstick sauté pan over high heat. Add the shiitake mushrooms and cook until browned and tender, about 5 minutes. Transfer to a cutting board.
2. Roughly chop the shiitake mushrooms and chickpeas and place in a large bowl. Add the curry powder, cumin, protein baking mix, water, and salt and pepper to taste and mix well. Form into 4 patties.
3. Transfer to a baking sheet and bake for 10 minutes to set the proteins in the patties. Grill them afterward if you would like, or eat as is.
4. Serve on protein buns garnished with the tomato, red onion, and carrots.

Tips: Look for Anita's coconut yogurt or AlternaSweets ketchup to finish your burgers.

PER SERVING
258 calories / 7g fat / 27g protein
23g carbohydrates / 11g fiber

Almond Veggie
Burger

Kiwi Veggie
Burger

Southwest Chili
Burger

CHAPTER 8

Mains

CUCUMBER NOODLES WITH CREAMY PESTO

MAKES 4 SERVINGS

I love pesto on anything, and this pesto is the besto. It's served over spiralized cucumbers, which have the perfect amount of crunch to satisfy. This dish is perfect for anyone—vegans, vegetarians, low-carb dieters, and even meat lovers will devour it, thanks to the addition of my rich cashew-cream sauce.

PREP TIME: 20 MINUTES
SOAK TIME: OVERNIGHT

INGREDIENTS

¼ cup raw cashews
1   cup packed basil leaves
1   tablespoon extra-virgin olive oil
2   tablespoons lemon juice
1   clove garlic
    Salt and pepper
2   English (seedless) cucumbers

METHOD

1. Place the cashews in a small container and add enough water to just cover. Transfer to the refrigerator to soak overnight.

2. Reserving the soaking water, drain the cashews and transfer to a blender. Add the basil, olive oil, lemon juice, and garlic and puree until the mixture achieves the texture of ricotta. If the mixture is dry, add some of the soaking liquid 1 tablespoon at a time until it comes together. Season the pesto with salt and pepper and set aside.

3. Using a mandoline with an ⅛-inch tooth attachment, shave the cucumbers into thin noodles. Place in a large bowl and pour the pesto sauce over the top. Mix well.

PER SERVING
139 calories / 11g fat / 3g protein
8g carbohydrates / 2.5g fiber

CAULIFLOWER STEAKS WITH RAW STEAK SAUCE

MAKES 4 SERVINGS

You're going to love the taste of grilled cauliflower, especially with my tomato sauce spooned over each steak. I'm not trying to turn cauliflower into a juicy rib-eye steak, trust me. I'm just giving you a different take on this versatile vegetable!

PREP TIME: 15 MINUTES
COOK TIME: 25 MINUTES

INGREDIENTS
1   tablespoon smoked paprika
1   tablespoon garlic powder
1   tablespoon onion powder
1   tablespoon ground cumin
1½ teaspoons chili powder
    Flesh of 2 tomatoes
½   teaspoon Worcestershire sauce
2   heads cauliflower
    Salt and pepper

METHOD
1. Preheat the oven to 375°F.
2. To make the spice rub, mix together the smoked paprika, garlic powder, onion powder, cumin, and chili powder. Set aside.
3. In a food processor, pulse the tomato flesh, 1 tablespoon of the spice rub, and the Worcestershire sauce until somewhat smooth, about 8 times. Set aside.
4. Cut the cauliflower vertically, through the stems, into 1-inch-thick slices. Do not remove the stem.
5. Dust the "steaks" liberally with the spice rub.
6. If you have a stovetop grill, grill the steaks for about 2 minutes on each side until browned. If you don't have a grill, set a sauté pan over high heat. When the pan is very hot, brown the steaks for about 90 seconds per side.
7. Place the browned steaks on a wire rack set over a baking sheet and place in the oven. Bake until tender, 20 to 25 minutes.
8. Place two or three cauliflower steaks on a plate. Sprinkle with salt and pepper. Spoon the sauce over the top.

PER SERVING
117 calories / 1g fat / 8g protein
25g carbohydrates / 10g fiber

CAULIFLOWER RISOTTO

MAKES 4 SERVINGS

Risotto is an Italian term describing a unique way to cook rice. Basically, the rice is cooked in broth or another liquid until it and the liquid swell to a creamy union. With this version of risotto, I use the same cooking method with cauliflower rice, thereby subtracting the calories and the carbs you'd get from rice.

PREP TIME: 10 MINUTES
COOK TIME: 20 MINUTES

INGREDIENTS

2 heads cauliflower, broken into florets
2 tablespoons extra-virgin olive oil
3 cloves garlic, thinly sliced
1½ cups vegetable stock
3 tablespoons grated Parmesan cheese
¼ cup chopped chives

METHOD

1. In a food processor, pulse the cauliflower florets 8 to 10 times, until it resembles small grains of rice.
2. Heat the olive oil in a large skillet over medium heat. Add the garlic and sweat until translucent, about 4 minutes.
3. Add the cauliflower and vegetable stock and cook until the cauliflower is softened and enough liquid has evaporated to make the mixture creamy, about 10 minutes.
4. Stir in the Parmesan and let sit 5 minutes to thicken. Finish by stirring in the chives.

PER SERVING
162 calories / 8g fat / 8g protein
19g carbohydrates / 7g fiber

VEGGIE PASTA POMODORO

MAKES 4 SERVINGS

Italians are champions of simple, classically delicious ways of using fresh tomatoes. And they should be; they've been cultivating them for hundreds of years. One of the many basic ways they prepare garden-fresh tomatoes is in a pomodoro sauce made with basil and garlic tossed with pasta (or in this case, spiralized vegetables).

PREP TIME: 20 MINUTES
COOK TIME: 15 MINUTES

INGREDIENTS

3 medium zucchini
3 medium yellow squash
  Salt
3 medium carrots
1 tablespoon extra-virgin olive oil
8 cloves garlic, thinly sliced
  Red chile flakes
24 basil leaves, torn
8 cups chopped tomatoes
¼ cup grated Parmesan cheese

METHOD

1. Cut the ends off of the zucchini, squash, and carrots. Using the instructions with your spiralizer, cut the vegetables into long angel hair–shaped pieces.
2. In a bowl, mix the squash and zucchini noodles together and lightly salt them. Set aside to drain.
3. Place the carrots on a microwave-safe plate and cover with plastic wrap. Microwave until softened, about 4 minutes. You will need to do this in two batches.
4. To make the pomodoro sauce: Heat the olive oil in a large sauté pan over medium heat. Add the garlic and cook until soft. Add the chile flakes and half of the basil and cook until fragrant, about 3 minutes. Add the tomatoes and cook until softened and beginning to fall apart, about 10 minutes.
5. Drain the liquid from the squash and zucchini. Place in a large bowl. Add the carrots and mix together.
6. Place a portion of the pasta on a microwave-safe plate and heat for 30 seconds to warm through. Repeat for all the portions. Top with the pomodoro sauce, the remaining basil, and the Parmesan.

PER SERVING
198 calories / 6g fat / 9g protein
32g carbohydrates / 10g fiber

CAULIFLOWER FRIED RICE

MAKES 4 SERVINGS

Here is a real-deal fried rice recipe—with one exception: Cauliflower rice subs for rice. Not that there's anything wrong with rice. It's nutritious and gluten-free. But if you're watching your carbs, cauliflower rice makes a delicious stand-in.

PREP TIME: 10 MINUTES
COOK TIME: 10 MINUTES

INGREDIENTS

2 heads cauliflower, broken into florets
2 medium carrots
1 tablespoon sesame oil
1 bunch scallions, chopped
⅓ cup reduced-sodium tamari
2 eggs, lightly beaten

METHOD

1. Pulse the cauliflower in a food processor until it resembles small grains of rice.
2. Shave the carrots into thin ribbons and set aside.
3. Heat the sesame oil in a large pot over high heat. Add the carrots and sauté until soft, about 3 minutes. Add the cauliflower rice and sauté until it begins to get soft, another 5 minutes. Add the scallions and cook for 1 minute.
4. Remove from the heat. Add the tamari and eggs and stir until the egg is cooked. Serve.

PER SERVING
226 calories / 10g fat / 13g protein
24g carbohydrates / 8g fiber

PROTEIN PASTA

MAKES 4 SERVINGS

PREP TIME: 5 MINUTES
COOK TIME: 15 MINUTES

INGREDIENTS

3   cups liquid egg whites
1   scoop protein powder
    (such as Rocco's Protein Powder Plus)
1   tablespoon psyllium husk powder

METHOD

1. Preheat the oven to 300°F. Line a rimmed baking sheet with a silicone baking mat.
2. In a blender, combine the egg whites, protein powder, and psyllium husk powder and blend on medium speed until just combined, about 15 seconds. Let sit 5 minutes for the mixture to thicken.
3. Pour the batter onto the lined baking sheet. Bake until the edges of the pasta begin to curl and the middle is firm, about 15 minutes. Let cool.
4. Use a knife or offset spatula to work the pasta sheet off the silicone mat. Roll the sheet as you would a cinnamon roll and cut crosswise to make pasta ribbons as wide as you would like.

PER SERVING
128 calories / <1g fat / 25g protein
6g carbohydrates / 4g fiber

MOROCCAN-STYLE BAKED FISH WITH CHICKPEAS AND MUSTARD GREENS

MAKES 4 SERVINGS

I love the flavors of Middle Eastern food, and Moroccan cuisine is one of my favorites. These snapper fillets are seasoned with *ras el hanout*, a traditional North African spice blend that includes cumin, cinnamon, and other warm, aromatic spices. Served with garlicky mustard greens and chickpeas, this is a meal that comes together easily but is sure to impress.

PREP TIME: 15 MINUTES
COOK TIME: 15 MINUTES

INGREDIENTS

1 pound mustard greens, ribs removed

2 cloves garlic, thinly shaved

½ cup chicken stock

4 skinless, boneless, red snapper fillets (1 to 1½ pounds)

1½ tablespoons ras el hanout

1 cup canned chickpeas, drained and rinsed

METHOD

1. Preheat the oven to 375°F. Line a baking sheet with parchment paper.
2. Roughly chop the mustard greens. In the largest pot you have, bring the garlic and chicken stock to a simmer. Add the mustard greens, cover, and cook until tender, 15 to 20 minutes.
3. As the greens near doneness, place the fish skin side down on the baking sheet. Season liberally with the *ras el hanout* and transfer to the oven. Cook until the fish is tender and flakes easily, about 7 minutes.
4. While the fish is in the oven, add the chickpeas to the mustard greens, to warm them through.
5. Divide the vegetable mixture among four plates and top with the cooked fish.

PER SERVING
226 calories / 2.5g fat / 34g protein
16g carbohydrates / 6.5g fiber

SALMON ESCABECHE

MAKES 4 SERVINGS

Escabeche is a Spanish dish of fish poached in vinegar, spices, and vegetables. It is usually served on toast, but I'm dispensing with the bread to keep it gluten-free. Plus, this method of cooking salmon is so flavorful that you don't need anything else! You can also serve the salmon cold over a plate of fresh greens with a light dressing.

PREP TIME: 10 MINUTES
COOK TIME: 25 MINUTES

INGREDIENTS

1   tablespoon extra-virgin olive oil
1   large onion, sliced
1   clove garlic, sliced
1   cup distilled white vinegar
1   cup water
6   packets Monk Fruit in the Raw
    Pinch of red chile flakes
¾   pound boneless, skinless wild salmon
    fillets

METHOD

1. Heat the olive oil in a large sauté pan over medium heat. Add the onion and sweat until soft and translucent, about 10 minutes. Add the garlic and sweat until soft, 2 to 3 minutes.
2. Add the vinegar, water, monk fruit, and chile flakes and bring to a boil. Place the salmon into the liquid and gently poach until the fish is tender and flakes easily, about 12 minutes. Cut the fish into 4 pieces.

Tips: This recipe works well with any fatty fish. Salmon works great on any kind of salad, and the poaching liquid makes a fantastic dressing.

PER SERVING
211 calories / 13g fat / 18g protein
6g carbohydrates / <1g fiber

GRAPE LEAF–WRAPPED MONKFISH WITH FENNEL

MAKES 4 SERVINGS

I've eaten fennel all my life, since it is often served raw as an appetizer during Christmas in Italian households. This fragrant licorice-flavored vegetable looks like celery with feathery fronds instead of leaves. It really enlivens this amazing fish entrée.

PREP TIME: 15 MINUTES
COOK TIME: 15 MINUTES

INGREDIENTS

3   tablespoons lemon juice
2   tablespoons extra-virgin olive oil
2   teaspoons za'atar (a Middle Eastern spice mix)
1   pound monkfish
8   grape leaves
2   fennel bulbs
2   tablespoons chopped dill

METHOD

1. Preheat the oven to 375°F.
2. In a small bowl, combine 1 tablespoon of the lemon juice, 1 tablespoon of the olive oil, and the za'atar.
3. Portion the fish into four 4-ounce portions. Place them in the za'atar marinade while you set up the grape leaves.
4. Arrange 2 grape leaves so that the stem ends slightly overlap. Center a piece of fish on the grape leaves and fold the sides of each leaf around the fish like a package. Move to a rimmed baking sheet. Repeat for each fish portion.
5. Wrap the top of the baking sheet with foil. Bake until the fish is tender and flakes easily, 13 to 15 minutes.
6. Meanwhile, shave the fennel as thinly as possible and place in ice water for 5 minutes, or until the fennel slices become rigid. Drain and transfer to a large bowl.
7. Toss with the remaining 2 tablespoons lemon juice, 1 tablespoon olive oil, and the dill.

PER SERVING
200 calories / 9g fat / 19g protein
12g carbohydrates / 4g fiber

SHRIMP CREOLE

MAKES 4 SERVINGS

In this classic Louisiana dish, the trio of onion, celery, and bell pepper forms the base of a flavorful tomato sauce that is then infused with hot sauce. You can easily double or triple this recipe to serve a crowd.

PREP TIME: 10 MINUTES
COOK TIME: 30 MINUTES

INGREDIENTS

1   tablespoon extra-virgin olive oil
2   cups chopped onions
1   cup chopped bell peppers
½   cup chopped celery
4   cups chopped tomatoes
1   tablespoon Worcestershire sauce
    Hot sauce
1   pound shrimp, peeled, including tails
1   cup chopped scallions

METHOD

1. Heat the olive oil in a large pot over medium heat. Add the onions, bell peppers, and celery and sweat until tender and translucent, about 10 minutes.
2. Add the tomatoes and cook until they have broken down and formed a thick sauce, about 15 minutes. Add the Worcestershire sauce and hot sauce to taste.
3. Reduce the heat to low. Add the shrimp and cook until they are just cooked through, about 3 minutes. Fold in the scallions and serve.

PER SERVING
225 calories / 6g fat / 26g protein
18g carbohydrates / 4g fiber

BOUILLABAISSE

MAKES 4 SERVINGS

Bouillabaisse is a delightful fish stew, and a very popular one in France. The vibrant colors of tomato and saffron, the stimulating flavors of fennel, onion, and garlic, all unite with clams, mussels, and shrimp to create a signature dish you can re-create in your own kitchen.

PREP TIME: 10 MINUTES
COOK TIME: 25 MINUTES

INGREDIENTS

1 tablespoon extra-virgin olive oil
1 cup sliced onions
¾ cup diced fennel
2 cloves garlic, sliced
2½ cups chopped tomatoes
  Pinch of saffron
3 cups seafood stock
12 littleneck clams
1 pound mussels
½ pound shrimp, heads and tails removed
  Salt and pepper

METHOD

1. Heat the oil in a large pot over medium heat. Add the onions and fennel and sweat until soft and translucent, about 7 minutes. Add the garlic and sweat another 3 minutes.
2. Add the tomatoes and cook until they start to become soft and release their juices, about 5 minutes.
3. Add the saffron and seafood stock and bring to a boil. Reduce the heat to medium-low. Place the clams and mussels in the pot, cover, and cook until the shells open, 3 to 5 minutes.
4. Uncover, reduce the heat to low, add the shrimp, and cook until the shrimp are just cooked through, about 2 minutes. Season with salt and pepper.

Tip: This recipe can be easily modified with any fresh fish from your fish market.

PER SERVING
232 calories / 7g fat / 26g protein
15g carbohydrates / 3g fiber

CHICKEN AND MUSHROOM EMPANADAS

MAKES 4 SERVINGS

Empanadas are meat-filled pastries that are easy to make and even easier to eat, because you can use your hands. You can change up the filling however you'd like—I made these using chicken, mushrooms, onions, and more—all wrapped up in gluten-free pizza dough. You can make them ahead of time and freeze them for future use. Empanadas make a great party dish.

PREP TIME: 20 MINUTES
COOK TIME: 40 MINUTES

INGREDIENTS

¾ pound boneless, skinless chicken breast
1   tablespoon extra-virgin olive oil
2   cups chopped onions
1   pound cremini mushrooms
1   teaspoon chili powder
    Pinch of red chile flakes
1½ cups chopped tomatoes
½ cup chopped cilantro
4   portions (52 grams each) store-bought gluten-free pizza dough (such as Gillian's)

METHOD

1. In a pot, combine the chicken with water just to cover. Bring to a boil and cook until cooked through, about 15 minutes. Drain and let cool, then pull apart with your hands. Set aside.

2. Preheat the oven to 350°F.

3. Heat the olive oil in a large skillet over medium heat. Add the onions and sweat until translucent, about 10 minutes. Increase the heat to high, add the mushrooms, and sauté until they begin to brown and soften, about 5 minutes.

4. Add the chili powder, chile flakes, tomatoes, and pulled chicken to the pot and cook until the mixture thickens, about 10 minutes. Finish the filling by stirring in the cilantro.

5. Meanwhile, roll each portion of pizza dough into a 12-inch round.

6. Divide the chicken and mushroom mixture evenly among the 4 rounds of dough. Use a spatula to fold the dough over the filling, then press the edges with your fingers to seal.

7. Transfer the empanadas to a baking sheet lined with parchment paper and bake until the crust is golden and crisp, about 10 minutes.

Tips: Keep cooked chicken ready to go in your refrigerator to cut down on prep time. Roll the pizza dough between two pieces of parchment. It is much easier to work with this way.

PER SERVING
302 calories / 8g fat / 27g protein
34g carbohydrates / 2.5g fiber

CHICKEN FAJITAS

MAKES 4 SERVINGS

———————

"Fajita" is a Tex-Mex term for "little strips" of beef skirt steak, the most common cut used to make fajitas, although a variety of fillings are now used. I've made these with chicken strips, accented by the traditional fajita veggies: onions and bell peppers. The filling goes into corn tortillas for a gluten-free Tex-Mex meal.

PREP TIME: 10 MINUTES
COOK TIME: 10 MINUTES

INGREDIENTS

1 pound boneless, skinless chicken breasts, cut into ½-inch-wide strips

1 onion, sliced

2 green bell peppers, cut into strips

2 teaspoons chili powder

1½ teaspoons garlic powder

¾ teaspoon ground cumin

1 tablespoon cornstarch

¼ cup unsalted chicken stock

1 tablespoon extra-virgin olive oil

8 corn tortillas

METHOD

1. In a large bowl, combine the chicken, onion, bell peppers, chili powder, garlic powder, cumin, cornstarch, and chicken stock and toss to coat well.

2. Heat the olive oil in a large pot over high heat. When it starts to smoke, add the chicken and vegetable mixture and stir vigorously until the vegetables soften and the chicken is cooked through, about 5 minutes. Remove from the heat and let stand for 5 minutes to allow the sauce to thicken.

3. Warm the tortillas by wrapping them in a damp towel and placing in the microwave for 30 seconds.

4. Divide the chicken mixture among the 8 tortillas and fold over.

PER SERVING
299 calories / 6g fat / 30g protein
31g carbohydrates / 5g fiber

GINGER ALE CHICKEN

MAKES 4 SERVINGS

Here's a fun way to bake a whole chicken. The usual recipe calls for a can of beer, but this one uses no-sugar ginger ale for the same moistening, flavor-packed effect.

PREP TIME: 10 MINUTES
COOK TIME: 40 MINUTES

INGREDIENTS

1   whole chicken (3 pounds)
1   tablespoon extra-virgin olive oil
    Salt and pepper
2   tablespoons fresh thyme leaves
1   can (6 ounces) stevia-sweetened ginger ale (such as Zevia)

METHOD

1. Preheat the oven to 400°F.
2. Brush the skin of the chicken with the olive oil. Season with salt and pepper and pat with the thyme leaves.
3. Pop open the ginger ale can and pour out about one-third of the soda. Place the can on a solid surface. Grab a chicken leg in each hand and plunk the bird cavity over the can. Stand it upright on a rimmed baking sheet.
4. Transfer to the oven and bake until the internal temperature is 165°F, about 40 minutes. Remove the chicken from the can and let rest before carving.

PER SERVING
371 calories / 20g fat / 44g protein
<1g carbohydrate / <1g fiber

FRIED CHICKEN WITH COLESLAW AND AVOCADO

MAKES 4 SERVINGS

Fried chicken is one of our best-loved comfort foods, but that greasy stuff is off limits if you're trying to keep a tight rein on your weight. In this recipe, I make fried chicken healthy and delicious through a technique known as flash-frying. Because the chicken is already cooked, it only needs to fry for 10 seconds on each side, as opposed to 10 to 15 minutes for traditional pan-frying or deep-frying. By spending so little time in the oil, the chicken and breading absorb far less of it, yet the outside still has time to fry up to a perfectly feather-light crunch.

PREP TIME: 20 MINUTES
COOK TIME: 10 MINUTES

INGREDIENTS

1 pound boneless, skinless chicken breast
½ cup buckwheat flour
2 eggs
½ cup almond meal
1½ teaspoons paprika
1½ teaspoons kosher salt
    Grapeseed oil, for flash-frying
1 bag (14 ounces) coleslaw mix
¼ cup apple cider vinegar
1 tablespoon extra-virgin olive oil
3 packets Monk Fruit in the Raw
2 avocados, cut in half

METHOD

1. Place the chicken in a microwave-safe container. Add enough water to cover halfway and cover with plastic wrap. Microwave until cooked through, 5 to 8 minutes (the cooking time will depend on the wattage of your microwave).

2. Cut the chicken into 1-inch-wide strips and set aside.

3. Set up a breading station: Place ¼ cup of the buckwheat flour in a shallow container. In a second container, beat the eggs. In a third, combine the remaining ¼ cup buckwheat flour, the almond meal, paprika, and salt.

4. Dip the chicken strips into the buckwheat flour, then into the egg, and then the buckwheat/almond mixture.

5. Pour ½ inch of grapeseed oil into a sauté pan. Heat until smoking, about 400°F. Flash-fry for 10 seconds on each side. Place on paper towels to rest.

6. In a large bowl, combine the coleslaw mix, vinegar, olive oil, and monk fruit and toss to coat.

7. To serve, divide the slaw among 4 plates. Top each with one-half of an avocado. Serve the fried chicken on the side.

PER SERVING
382 calories / 21g fat / 28g protein
24g carbohydrates / 10g fiber

ALMOND RICOTTA AND OLIVE STUFFED CHICKEN

MAKES 4 SERVINGS

Three-ingredient recipes—is anything better? I love the combination of chicken stuffed with creamy almond ricotta and salty Kalamata olives. My take on "stuffed chicken" is light on calories but heavy on flavor—and won't leave you feeling uncomfortably "stuffed"!

PREP TIME: 20 MINUTES
COOK TIME: 15 MINUTES

INGREDIENTS

¼   cup raw almonds
¼   cup Kalamata olives, pitted
1   pound boneless, skinless chicken breast, sliced to serve

METHOD

1. Preheat the oven to 400°F.
2. In a small heatproof bowl, pour boiling water over the almonds to just cover. Let soak for 30 to 60 minutes.
3. Reserving the soaking water, drain the almonds and transfer to a food processor. Add the olives and pulse until the mixture achieves the texture of ricotta. If the mixture is dry, add some of the soaking liquid 1 tablespoon at a time until it comes together.
4. Cut a horizontal slit into each chicken breast and open them up. Divide the almond ricotta evenly among the breasts. Close the chicken up and tie with butcher twine.
5. Transfer to a baking sheet and bake until the internal temperature is 165°F, about 15 minutes.

Tip: This dish would be delicious atop the Cauliflower Risotto (page 176).

PER SERVING
196 calories / 7.5g fat / 28g protein
3g carbohydrates / 1g fiber

CHICKEN TIKKA MASALA

MAKES 4 SERVINGS

Tikka masala has mysterious origins, with some claiming that it was first created in an Indian restaurant in Scotland! Whatever its origins, this delicious dish features chunks of chicken cooked in various sauces seasoned with a spice mixture (masala), and usually involves cream. I've chosen to make mine in a rich, tomato-based sauce without the dairy.

PREP TIME: 15 MINUTES
COOK TIME: 20 MINUTES

INGREDIENTS

1   tablespoon extra-virgin olive oil
1   cup half-moon slices white onion
2   tablespoons garam masala
2   tablespoons tomato paste
1   pound boneless, skinless chicken breasts, cut into bite-size pieces
4   medium tomatoes, diced
1   cup chicken stock

METHOD

1. Heat the olive oil in a large pot over medium heat. Add the onion and sweat until translucent, about 5 minutes. Add the garam masala and tomato paste. Cook until fragrant, about 2 minutes.

3. Increase the heat to high, add the chicken, and cook until browned. Add the tomatoes and cook until they begin to break down and release their juices, about 5 minutes. Add the chicken stock and cook until the sauce thickens, another 5 to 10 minutes.

PER SERVING
207 calories / 5g fat / 28g protein
11g carbohydrates / 2g fiber

ROASTED CORNISH GAME HENS

MAKES 4 SERVINGS

———————————

Why did the Cornish game hen cross the road? To let everyone know they exist and are a great alternative for people who don't like turkey. These hens are young chickens that are a cross between Cornish gamecocks and Plymouth rock hens. You can stuff them with anything you want, including conventional stuffing. I've chosen to keep it simple with a stuffing of veggies and herbs.

PREP TIME: 10 MINUTES
COOK TIME: 30 MINUTES

INGREDIENTS

4   Cornish game hens (about 1½ pounds each)
1   medium onion, quartered
1   large stalk celery, cut in half, plus more for the roasting pan
4   sprigs rosemary
2   tablespoons extra-virgin olive oil
    Salt and pepper

METHOD

1. Preheat the oven to 400°F.
2. Stuff the cavities of the hens with the onion, celery, and rosemary. Brush the outsides of each with the olive oil and season with salt and pepper.
3. Make a makeshift rack on a rimmed baking sheet by resting the hens on pieces of celery. Transfer to the oven and bake until the skin is crisp and the internal temperature is 165°F, about 30 minutes.
4. Let rest before serving.

PER SERVING
240 calories / 20g fat / 15g protein
0g carbohydrate / 0g fiber

STUFFED ZUCCHINI

MAKES 4 SERVINGS

If your garden produces a bumper crop of zucchini every year, this recipe is a great way to use it up. I've scooped out zucchini halves and packed them with a mixture of ground turkey and vegetables—and the result is magic.

PREP TIME: 30 MINUTES
COOK TIME: 1 HOUR

INGREDIENTS

4   large zucchini
1   tablespoon extra-virgin olive oil
2   cups diced onions
1   cup diced celery
1   cup diced carrots
1   pound lean ground turkey
1   tablespoon ras el hanout
2   tablespoons tomato paste
3   cups chopped tomatoes
½   cup chopped cilantro

METHOD

1. Preheat the oven to 375°F.
2. Halve the zucchini lengthwise and use a spoon to scoop out the insides. Reserve the innards. Place the hollowed-out zucchini on a baking sheet.
3. Heat the oil in a large pot. Add the onions, celery, and carrots and sweat until soft and translucent, about 10 minutes.
4. Increase the heat to high, add the turkey, and brown for about 5 minutes. Add the *ras el hanout*, tomato paste, tomatoes, and reserved zucchini insides and cook until everything is soft and the mixture is almost dry. Finish with the cilantro.
6. Spoon the stuffing into the zucchini halves and bake until the zucchini is soft, 45 minutes to 1 hour.

PER SERVING
316 calories / 14g fat / 27g protein
25g carbohydrates / 7g fiber

ITALIAN SLOPPY JOES

MAKES 4 SERVINGS

The popular sloppy joe was created by a cook named Joe in 1930 at a Sioux City, Iowa, café, and was first described as a loose meat sandwich. Since then, it's been a popular sandwich in homes and restaurants everywhere. My version goes Italian, thanks to the addition of garlic, basil, and oregano.

PREP TIME: 10 MINUTES
COOK TIME: 20 MINUTES

INGREDIENTS

4 portobello mushrooms
1 tablespoon extra-virgin olive oil
1 cup diced onion
1 clove garlic, finely chopped
1 pound lean ground turkey
2 tablespoons tomato paste
3 cups chopped tomatoes
¼ cup chopped basil
1½ teaspoons oregano leaves, chopped

METHOD

1. Preheat the oven to 400°F.
2. Remove the stems from the portobellos. Place the mushrooms gill side up on a baking sheet, transfer to the oven, and roast until they are browned and just tender, about 10 minutes.
3. Meanwhile, heat the olive oil in a large sauté pan over medium heat. Add the onion and sweat until translucent, about 10 minutes.
4. Add the garlic and cook another 3 minutes. Increase the heat to high, add the turkey, and cook until browned.
5. Add the tomato paste and tomatoes and cook until a thick sauce is formed and you can see the bottom of the pan when you stir the turkey mixture.
6. Finish with the chopped basil and oregano. Serve atop the roasted mushroom caps.

PER SERVING
271 calories / 14g fat / 25g protein
14g carbohydrates / 4g fiber

TURKEY SLIDERS WITH TOMATO JAM

MAKES 4 SERVINGS

For light snacks or sports-watching treats, some good old artery-clogging, fat-packing standbys are sure to please. But why not try some healthier finger-food options? Instead of beef sliders with cheese, for example, try my turkey sliders with their special jam, all wrapped in large lettuce leaves.

PREP TIME: 15 MINUTES
COOK TIME: 1 HOUR

INGREDIENTS

4   cups chopped tomatoes
2   tablespoons tomato paste
1   tablespoon apple cider vinegar
3   packets Monk Fruit in the Raw
1   cup puffed rice cereal
½   cup water
1   pound lean ground turkey
    Salt and pepper
8   butter lettuce leaves

METHOD

1. Cook the chopped tomatoes in a medium saucepan over medium-high heat until they are broken down, thickened, and most of the liquid has evaporated. Stir in the tomato paste, vinegar, and monk fruit. Set the tomato jam aside.

2. In a large bowl, combine the puffed rice and water and use your hands to break up the puffs. Add the ground turkey, season with salt and pepper, and mix well to combine. Form into 8 slider-size patties and place in the freezer for 10 to 15 minutes to firm up.

3. Grill the sliders until well cooked, about 5 minutes per side. Transfer to a plate to rest.

4. To serve, place a slider in the center of a lettuce leaf, top with the tomato jam, and wrap the leaf around it like a package.

PER SERVING
233 calories / 10g fat / 24g protein
14g carbohydrates / 3g fiber

TURKEY, SPINACH, AND RED ONION BURGERS

MAKES 4 SERVINGS

Each one of these burgers is a meal all by itself, because spinach, onion, and garlic are incorporated into the patty. That's a lot of nutrition packed into a burger! But to really complete the meal, I'd suggest serving these delicious burgers with one of my side slaws.

PREP TIME: 15 MINUTES
COOK TIME: 10 MINUTES

INGREDIENTS

1   clove garlic, smashed with a meat mallet
10 ounces spinach
1   cup finely chopped red onion
1   pound lean ground turkey
½   cup rolled oats

METHOD

1. Preheat the oven to 400°F.
2. Place a large sauté pan over high heat. Add the garlic and spinach and cook to wilt. Drain on a paper towel.
3. Roughly chop the spinach mixture and add to a large bowl.
4. Add the onion, turkey, and oats to the bowl and mix with your hands until just combined. Portion into 4 balls.
5. Place a large sauté pan over high heat and coat with cooking spray. When the pan is very hot, add the burgers and smash them flat with your hand or a spatula. Cook until a crust has formed on one side. Flip and brown the other side.
6. Place on a baking sheet, transfer to the oven, and cook until the patties are cooked through, about 5 minutes.

Tips: Make sure you get rolled oats for this and not instant. These also work great on the grill. Just flatten the patties beforehand.

PER SERVING
229 calories / 9g fat / 26g protein
13g carbohydrates / 3g fiber

ROASTED TURKEY BREAST WITH GRAVY

MAKES 4 SERVINGS

I don't just love it, but live for it. And much of that is thanks to my wonderful childhood memories of Thanksgiving. But as I've gotten older, there's something I have come to not love about Thanksgiving dinner—all those calories. They make you want to crash on the couch, loosen your belt, and doze off into a food coma. A nice indulgence, but not a healthy lifestyle. To scale things down, I've used turkey breast and a delicious low-fat gravy. This recipe will satisfy anyone in your family for just 185 calories and 5 grams of fat.

PREP TIME: 10 MINUTES
COOK TIME: 25 MINUTES

INGREDIENTS

1   tablespoon extra-virgin olive oil
1   pound boneless, skinless turkey breast
4   cups low-sodium chicken stock
2   tablespoons kudzu powder
    Salt and pepper

METHOD

1. Preheat the oven to 400°F.
2. Heat the olive oil in a large sauté pan over high heat. When the oil begins to smoke, gently place the turkey breast in the pan. Cook both sides until browned, about 3 minutes per side.
3. Transfer to a baking sheet, place in the oven, and roast until the internal temperature is 165°F, about 10 minutes. Let rest, then slice.
3. Meanwhile, deglaze the sauté pan with 3½ cups of the chicken stock and scrape the bottom to remove any stuck-on bits. Cook to reduce the liquid by half.
4. Stir the kudzu into the remaining chicken stock until it dissolves and add to the reduced chicken stock. Stir constantly until the stock returns to a boil and thickens. Season the gravy with salt and pepper and serve.

PER SERVING
185 calories / 5g fat / 29g protein
3g carbohydrates / 0g fiber

CRANBERRY SAUCE

MAKES 4 SERVINGS

I used to recommend cranberry sauce made with agave syrup. But I found that even those products contained too much sugar. So I decided to invent my own sugar-free cranberry sauce, sweetened up with orange juice and monk fruit. Enjoy!

PREP TIME: 5 MINUTES
COOK TIME: 40 MINUTES

INGREDIENTS

½   pound cranberries

2   tablespoons grated orange zest

¼   cup orange juice

8   packets Monk Fruit in the Raw
    Salt and pepper

METHOD

In a small saucepan, combine the cranberries, orange zest, orange juice, monk fruit, and salt and pepper to taste. Cook over medium heat until the cranberries burst and the mixture becomes thick and dry, about 40 minutes.

PER SERVING

34 calories / 0g fat / <1g protein
9g carbohydrates / 3g fiber

ROSEMARY PORK LOIN

MAKES 4 SERVINGS

Please, I beg of you: Do not overcook this pork tenderloin. It's a very forgiving cut, so it will be delicious no matter what, but if it's cooked properly, it will be sublime!

PREP TIME: 5 MINUTES
COOK TIME: 15 MINUTES

INGREDIENTS

1   pound pork tenderloin, trimmed of fat
    Salt and pepper
1   tablespoon extra-virgin olive oil
1   tablespoon apple cider vinegar
1   tablespoon Dijon mustard
1   clove garlic, thinly sliced
1   tablespoon rosemary leaves

METHOD

1. Preheat the oven to 400°F. Season the pork with salt and pepper.
2. Heat the olive oil in a large sauté pan over high heat. When the oil just begins to smoke, add the pork and brown on three sides, about 2 minutes per side. Transfer to a cutting board.
3. In a small bowl, stir together the vinegar and mustard. Coat the pork in the mixture.
4. Using a paring knife, cut slits into the length of the pork and place a slice of garlic into each one. Sprinkle the pork with the rosemary and bake on a rimmed baking sheet or in a casserole for about 5 minutes to finish cooking.
5. Remove from the oven and let rest for 10 minutes before slicing.

Tip: This cooking time should get you pork that is cooked to medium. Cook longer if you want it more done.

PER SERVING
172 calories / 7g fat / 26g protein
1g carbohydrate / <1g fiber

PORK CHOPS WITH PEPPER SAUCE

MAKES 4 SERVINGS

Pork chops smothered in a peppery sauce is nothing new, but delivering it in 20 minutes and at under 200 calories per serving is. Like most meats, pork can get dry and tough if overcooked. I think people are so afraid of eating undercooked meat that they tend to compensate by cooking the life (along with the flavor and tenderness) right out of it. So follow my timing directions, then stop! Really!

PREP TIME: 5 MINUTES
COOK TIME: 15 MINUTES

INGREDIENTS

1 tablespoon extra-virgin olive oil
1 pound lean pork chops, at least four chops
4 teaspoons cornstarch
14 ounces reduced-sodium pork or beef broth
½ teaspoon black pepper

METHOD

1. Heat the olive oil in a large sauté pan over high heat. Add the pork chops and brown for about 3 minutes on each side. Transfer to a baking sheet to rest.
2. In a bowl, stir the cornstarch into the pork broth.
3. Drain the oil from the sauté pan and return to medium heat. Deglaze the pan with the stock and whisk until the stock boils and thickens. Season with the pepper.

PER SERVING
181 calories / 6g fat / 27g protein
3g carbohydrates / <1g fiber

"MEAT AND TWO" VEG BALLS WITH MUSTARD SAUCE

MAKES 4 SERVINGS

This is my take on the popular Southern concept of "meat and three"— in this case, all rolled up into one "ball." If you want to sneak more veggies into your diet or that of your family, this recipe will do the trick!

PREP TIME: 15 MINUTES
COOK TIME: 15 MINUTES

INGREDIENTS

1   cup puffed rice cereal
¼   cup beef broth
1   pound lean ground beef
2   cups grated carrots (shaved on the large holes of a box grater)
⅓   cup frozen peas
2   tablespoons Colman's mustard powder
¼   cup full-fat coconut milk
1   cup unsweetened coconut milk beverage (such as So Delicious)
1   tablespoon extra-virgin olive oil
    Salt and pepper

METHOD

1. Place the puffed rice in a large bowl. Pour the beef broth over the top and mix well to break up the puffs. Add the ground beef, grated carrots, and frozen peas, mix well to combine, and form into 16 meatballs. Place in the freezer.

2. In a small bowl, whisk together the mustard powder and both coconut milks.

3. Heat the olive oil in a skillet over high heat. Remove the meatballs from the freezer, add to the pan, and brown on at least three sides. Remove the meatballs from the pan.

4. Pour in the coconut milk mixture and bring to a boil, scraping the bottom of the pan while whisking. Once the mixture boils, return the meatballs to the pan, cover, reduce the heat to low, and cook until the meatballs are fully cooked, about 10 minutes. Season with salt and pepper.

PER SERVING
305 calories / 18g fat / 26g protein
13g carbohydrates / 2g fiber

GINGER-SOY KOFTA AND TOMATO SALAD

MAKES 4 SERVINGS

It's not just us Italians who love our meatballs. Let me introduce you to *kofta*, a particularly flavorful variety of meatball generally found in the Middle East and India. You'll serve them atop a fresh salad of tomatoes, scallions, and cucumbers.

PREP TIME: 15 MINUTES
COOK TIME: 15 MINUTES

INGREDIENTS

1   cup puffed rice cereal
¼   cup low-sodium beef broth
1   tablespoon grated fresh ginger
2   tablespoons reduced-sodium tamari
1   pound lean ground beef
1½ cups chopped scallions
1   cup cherry tomatoes, halved
1   cucumber, chopped
1   tablespoon sesame oil
2   tablespoons lemon juice

METHOD

1. Preheat the broiler.
2. In a small bowl, combine the puffed rice, beef broth, ginger, and tamari. Stir with a spoon or rubber spatula to break up the puffed rice.
3. Place the ground beef in a large bowl. Add the puffed rice mixture and 1 cup of the scallions and mix well.
4. To form the koftas, divide the beef into 8 equal portions and shape each into a football shape with your hands. Transfer to a baking sheet.
5. Place under the broiler and cook until the outside is crisp and browned and the internal temperature is 160°F, 12 to 15 minutes.
6. Meanwhile, in a large bowl, combine the remaining ½ cup scallions, the tomatoes, cucumber, sesame oil, and lemon juice and mix well.
7. Transfer the vegetables to 4 serving bowls. Place the kofta on top of the salad and serve.

PER SERVING
240 calories / 8g fat / 27g protein
13g carbohydrates / 2g fiber

ESPRESSO MEATLOAF

MAKES 4 SERVINGS

—————

Espresso in meatloaf? Yes, just 2 teaspoons of espresso powder in the topping to amplify the beefy flavor of meatloaf. This recipe is gluten-free, too, since it uses puffed rice (instead of bread) as a binder.

PREP TIME: 10 MINUTES
COOK TIME: 30 MINUTES

INGREDIENTS

1   cup puffed rice cereal
½   cup reduced-sodium beef broth
1   pound lean ground beef
    Salt and pepper
2   tablespoons unsweetened ketchup
2   tablespoons tomato paste
1   teaspoon Worcestershire sauce
2   teaspoons instant espresso powder (such as Medaglia d'Oro)

METHOD

1. Preheat the oven to 375°F.
2. Place the puffed rice in a large bowl. Pour the beef broth on top of it and mix well to break apart the puffs.
3. Add the ground beef and mix well. Season with salt and pepper. Form into a 7 x 4-inch loaf shape and place on a baking sheet. Transfer to the oven and bake for 25 minutes. Remove from the oven and turn the broiler to high.
4. In a small bowl, mix together the ketchup, tomato paste, Worcestershire sauce, and espresso powder. Brush this over the meatloaf and return to the broiler. Check after 5 minutes. The crust of the meatloaf should be browned and sticky to the touch.

PER SERVING
205 calories / 8g fat / 25g protein
7g carbohydrates / <1g fiber

GRILLED SIRLOIN WITH ASPARAGUS

MAKES 4 SERVINGS

Even though I've cut back a bit on meat, life without beef would be . . . depressing. Plus, beef is a healthy choice—it's high in protein, B vitamins, iron, zinc, and other minerals. And when the right cuts are trimmed of any visible fat, it can be nearly as lean as a boneless, skinless chicken breast.

PREP TIME: 10 MINUTES
COOK TIME: 15 MINUTES

INGREDIENTS

1   tablespoon grapeseed oil
1   pound beef sirloin
2   cloves garlic, crushed
1½ tablespoons thyme leaves
2   bunches asparagus, trimmed and peeled
2   tablespoons champagne vinegar
¼   cup water

METHOD

1. Preheat the oven to 400°F.
2. Heat the grapeseed oil in a large sauté pan over high heat until very hot. Add the sirloin, garlic, and thyme and cook until one side is browned and releases from the pan readily, about 3 minutes. Flip and cook another 3 minutes. Discard the garlic, transfer to a baking sheet, and move to the oven to finish, about 5 minutes for medium-rare.
3. In the pan used to brown the steak, add the asparagus, vinegar, and water. Cook over high heat until the asparagus is softened and browned, about 5 minutes.
4. Remove the steak from oven, and allow to rest for 10 minutes before slicing. Serve with the asparagus.

PER SERVING
290 calories / 18g fat / 26g protein
6g carbohydrates / 3g fiber

STEAK WITH BALSAMIC BBQ SAUCE

MAKES 4 SERVINGS

With the tender flank steak and intensely flavored BBQ sauce, this dish will make a healthy, memorable impact and leave you feeling satiated and energized.

PREP TIME: 10 MINUTES
COOK TIME: 10 MINUTES

INGREDIENTS

1 pound flank steak
   Salt and pepper
2 tablespoons tomato paste
2 tablespoons unsweetened ketchup
1 tablespoon balsamic vinegar
¼ teaspoon chili powder

METHOD

1. Prepare a grill.
2. Season the flank steak with salt and pepper and grill for about 3 minutes per side for medium-rare. Let rest before slicing.
3. While the steak is resting, in a small bowl, combine the tomato paste, ketchup, vinegar, and chili powder.
4. Brush the steak with the BBQ mixture and slice.

PER SERVING
171 calories / 6g fat / 25g protein
3g carbohydrates / <1g fiber

CHAPTER 9

Bites & Snacks

RAW STUFFED MUSHROOMS

MAKES 4 SERVINGS

One of my favorite go-to appetizers is stuffed mushrooms. Usually, I would bake them, but this raw version, stuffed with walnuts, tomatoes, and basil, is delectable.

PREP TIME: 20 MINUTES

INGREDIENTS

12 cremini mushrooms
    Salt and pepper
¼   cup walnuts, chopped
1   cup finely diced tomatoes
¼   cup basil leaves, chopped
1   tablespoon extra-virgin olive oil
¼   cup balsamic vinegar

METHOD

1. Reserving the stems, trim the mushroom caps. Season the caps with salt and pepper and set aside.
2. Chop the mushroom stems and place them in a bowl. Add the walnuts, tomatoes, basil, olive oil, and vinegar and toss to combine.
3. Spoon this mixture into the mushroom caps and serve.

PER SERVING
101 calories / 8g fat / 4g protein
6g carbohydrates / 1g fiber

BEET TARTARE

MAKES 4 SERVINGS

If you've never been much for raw beef (beef tartare) or raw tuna (tuna tartare), here's your chance to plunge into the world of tartare—but with raw veggies only. The centerpiece ingredient is the nutritious, hearty beet, made exceptionally delicious with the addition of Dijon mustard and horseradish.

PREP TIME: 20 MINUTES

INGREDIENTS

1   pound beets
1   tablespoon prepared horseradish
1½ teaspoons Dijon mustard
     Juice of 1 lemon
1½ teaspoons Worcestershire sauce
1   teaspoon extra-virgin olive oil
¼   cup chopped Italian flat parsley

METHOD

1. Grate the beets on the large holes of a box grater or with the grater attachment in a food processor.
2. Place in a large bowl and stir in the horseradish, mustard, lemon juice, Worcestershire sauce, and olive oil. Let stand for 10 minutes.
3. Stir in the parsley and serve.

PER SERVING
71 calories / 2g fat / 2g protein
13g carbohydrates / 4g fiber

RAW CHARD TACOS

MAKES 4 SERVINGS

PREP TIME: 20 MINUTES

INGREDIENTS

½ head cauliflower

½ teaspoon chili powder

1 tablespoon extra-virgin olive oil

1½ teaspoons apple cider vinegar
   Salt and pepper

4 large rainbow chard leaves

6 ounces cherry tomatoes, halved

1 cup sliced cucumber

½ cup sliced cremini mushrooms

METHOD

1. Using the large holes on a box grater, shave the cauliflower to make "rice." Place in a medium bowl and add the chili powder, olive oil, and vinegar. Season with salt and pepper and stir to combine.

2. Using a small knife, shave down any large ribs in the chard. Cut the leaves crosswise, in half.

3. Divide the rice mixture, cherry tomatoes, cucumber, and mushrooms among the chard taco "shells."

Tip: This recipe works well with any fresh vegetables from your local farmers' market.

PER SERVING
72 calories / 4g fat / 3g protein
9g carbohydrates / 3g fiber

BASS CRUDO WITH TOMATILLOS

MAKES 4 SERVINGS

PREP TIME: 15 MINUTES

INGREDIENTS

1   cup diced tomatillos

1   tablespoon minced jalapeños (seeded and deribbed)

¼   cup chopped cilantro

¼   cup lime juice

1   tablespoon olive oil

¾   pound boneless, skinless black bass fillets

METHOD

1. In a small bowl, combine the tomatillos, jalapeños, cilantro, lime juice, and olive oil and mix well.
2. Slice the bass into ¼-inch-thick slices and arrange on plates. Pour the tomatillo mixture over the fish and serve.

PER SERVING
119 calories / 6g fat / 15g protein
2g carbohydrates / <1g fiber

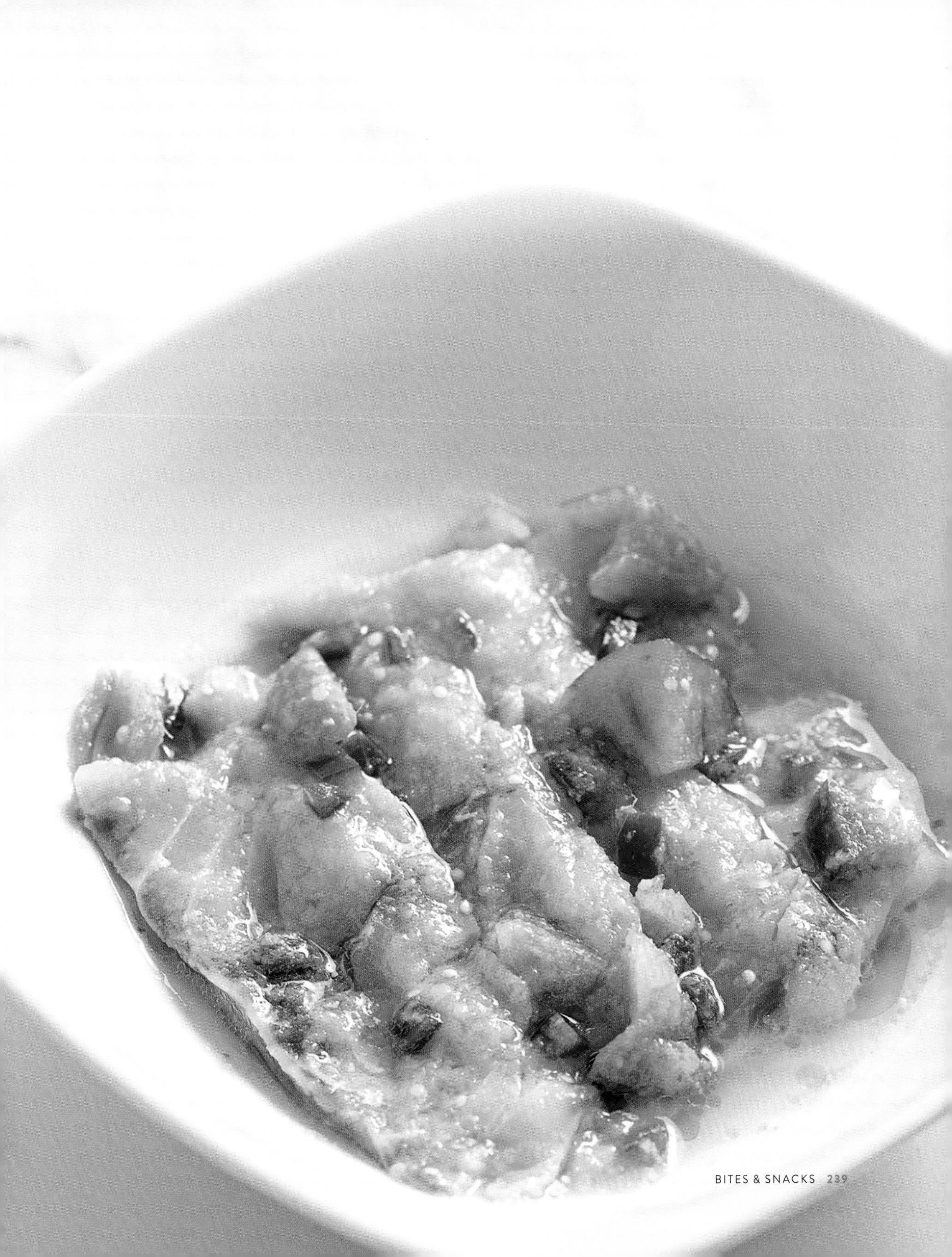

SALMON CRUDO WITH LEMON CHIA

MAKES 4 SERVINGS

———————————

PREP TIME: 20 MINUTES
SOAK TIME: OVERNIGHT

INGREDIENTS

¼ cup lemon juice

½ teaspoon chia seeds

1 tablespoon grated fresh ginger
Salt and pepper

¾ pound boneless, skinless wild salmon
fillet, cut into ¼-inch-thick slices

½ cup cilantro leaves

METHOD

1. In a small bowl, combine the lemon juice, chia seeds, ginger, salt and pepper to taste and refrigerate overnight to hydrate.

2. Place the sliced salmon on serving dishes, spoon the lemon juice/chia mixture over the top, and garnish with the cilantro.

PER SERVING

164 calories / 9g fat / 17g protein

2g carbohydrates / <1g fiber

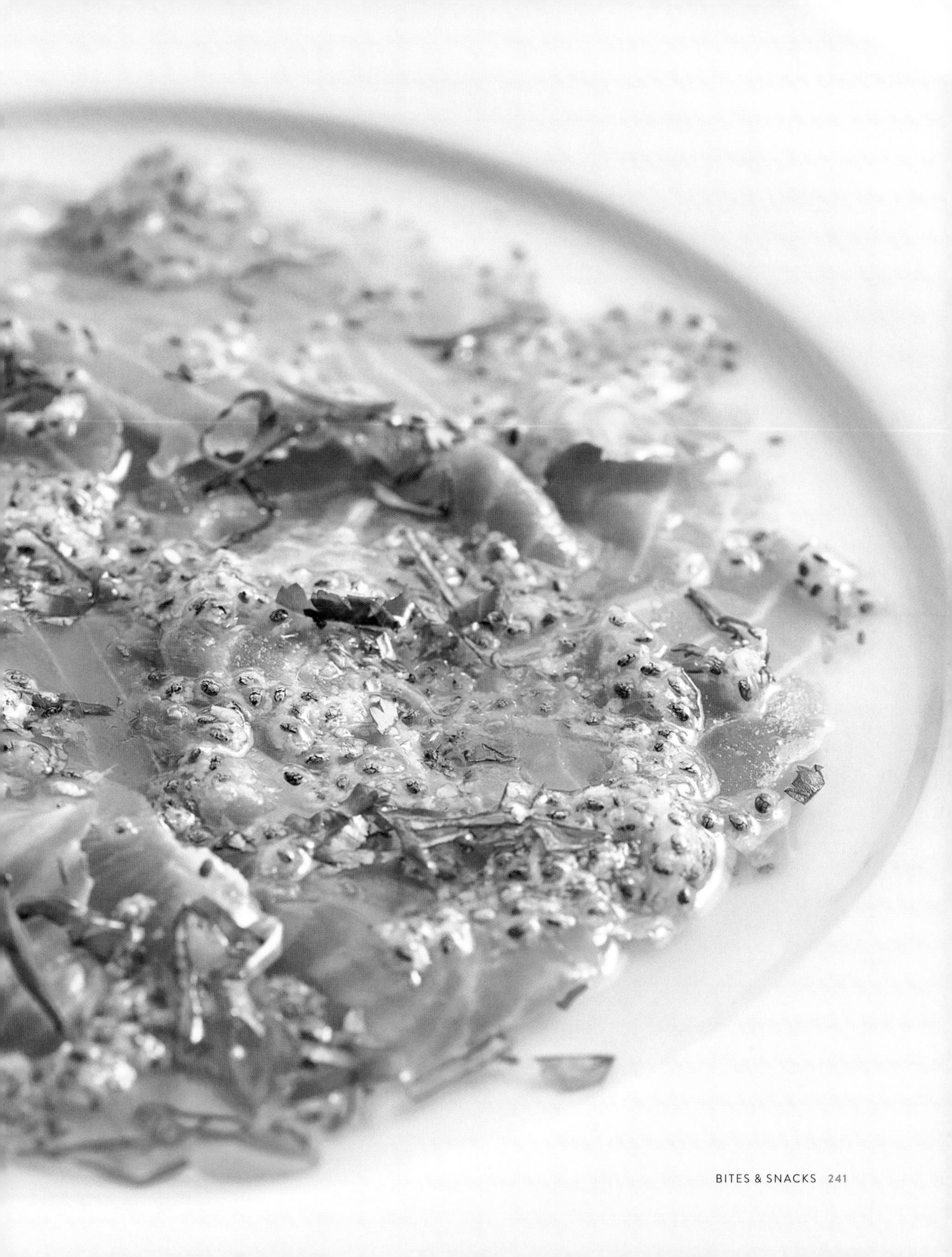

TUNA POKE CARPACCIO

MAKES 4 SERVINGS

———————

Poke is a Hawaiian verb for to slice or to cut, and this fish salad is native to the Hawaiian Islands. Poke restaurants have begun to pop up in the rest of the country lately, and this simple, healthy dish is on track to become as popular as sushi!

PREP TIME: 20 MINUTES

INGREDIENTS

¾ pound sushi-grade tuna, cut into ¼-inch-thick slices

4 teaspoons reduced-sodium tamari

1 teaspoon sesame oil

3 tablespoons thinly sliced scallions

½ sheet nori, sliced into strips

METHOD

1. Divide the tuna into 4 equal portions (3 ounces each). Place a portion of tuna slices between two pieces of plastic wrap and flatten with the smooth side of a meat mallet. Remove one piece of plastic and transfer to a serving plate. Repeat for the remaining 3 portions.

2. In a small bowl, mix together the tamari and sesame oil and sprinkle over the top of the tuna. Garnish with the scallions and nori.

PER SERVING

120 calories / 2g fat / 22g protein

1g carbohydrate / 28g fiber

SHRIMP AND SCALLOP CEVICHE

MAKES 4 SERVINGS

————————

Ceviche is prepared by marinating raw seafood in citrus juices, such as lemon or lime. I love it as an alternative to sushi because it's so simple to prepare. It's one of the most refreshing and delicious appetizers you can make.

PREP TIME: 15 MINUTES
COOK TIME: 1 MINUTE
SOAK TIME: 15 MINUTES

INGREDIENTS

1   medium cucumber, chopped

1   small stalk lemongrass, chopped

2½ tablespoons grated fresh ginger

1   cup lime juice

½   pound shrimp, peeled with tails removed

½   pound bay scallops

½   cup diced grapefruit

¼   cup cilantro leaves, sliced

METHOD

1. In a blender, combine the cucumber, lemongrass, and ginger and puree on high until smooth, about 30 seconds. Strain the juices into a bowl (discard the solids).

2. Whisk the lime juice into the cucumber juice and set aside.

3. Set up a bowl of ice and water. Bring a small pot of water to a boil. Add the shrimp to the boiling water and blanch for 15 seconds to set the color. Remove and shock in the ice bath. Drain and cut into bite-size pieces.

4. Place the shrimp and scallops in the lime/cucumber juice and mix well. Set aside for 15 minutes, or until the ceviche has reached a texture you like. Stir in the grapefruit and cilantro and serve.

PER SERVING
145 calories / 2g fat / 22g protein
15g carbohydrates / <1g fiber

ASIAN-STYLE CEVICHE

MAKES 4 SERVINGS

A traditional dish from South America, ceviche is an alternative to sashimi that is easy to prepare and can be made with a variety of seafood. For this dish I've chosen delicious omega-3–rich salmon—wild-caught of course—topped with avocado.

PREP TIME: 20 MINUTES
COOK TIME: 5 MINUTES

INGREDIENTS

- ½ pound boneless, skinless wild salmon fillet
- 2 tablespoons grated fresh ginger
- 1 cup chopped scallions
- 1 avocado
- 2 tablespoons lime juice
- ¼ cup sesame oil
- 2 tablespoons reduced-sodium tamari

METHOD

1. With a very sharp knife, slice the salmon as thinly as possible. Lay it out in a single layer on 4 plates. Sprinkle it with the ginger and scallions.
2. Mash the avocado with the lime juice and set aside.
3. In a small pot, warm the oil through. Pour the oil over the salmon and top with the tamari and avocado.

PER SERVING
354 calories / 28g fat / 19g protein
6g carbohydrates / 2.5g fiber

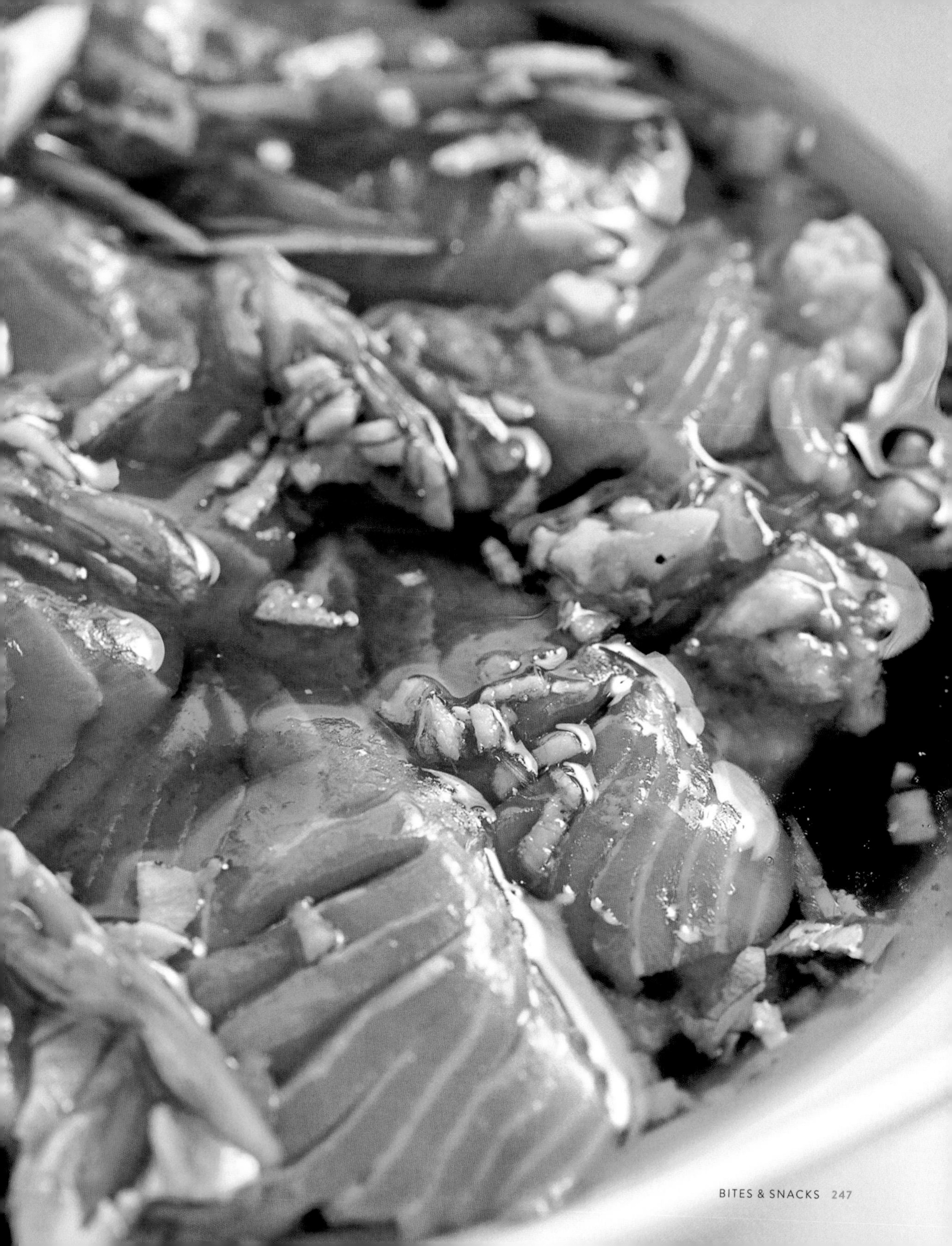

CEVICHE WITH LECHE DE TIGRE

MAKES 4 SERVINGS

PREP TIME: 15 MINUTES
SOAK TIME: 5 MINUTES

INGREDIENTS

½ cup lime juice

⅓ cup thinly sliced red onion
   Red chile flakes

2 tablespoons grated fresh ginger
   Salt and pepper

¾ pound fluke, cut into ¼-inch-thick slices

¼ cup fresh corn kernels

½ cup cilantro leaves

PER SERVING
108 calories / 2g fat / 16g protein
6g carbohydrates / <1g fiber

METHOD

1. In a medium bowl, combine the lime juice, red onion, chile flakes to taste, the ginger, and salt and pepper to taste and stir to combine.

2. Add the fluke and mix well to coat the fish. Set aside for 5 minutes.

3. Stir the corn into the fluke mixture.

4. To serve, the liquid can be drained off this dish and served in a glass on the side, or you can portion everything into 4 bowls. Serve topped with the cilantro.

TZATZIKI

MAKES 4 SERVINGS

PREP TIME: 15 MINUTES

INGREDIENTS

2   medium cucumbers, roughly chopped
⅓   cup unsweetened nondairy coconut
     yogurt (such as So Delicious)
1   clove garlic, finely grated
     Juice of 2 lemons
2   tablespoons chopped dill
1   scoop protein powder
     (such as Rocco's Protein Powder Plus)
     Salt

METHOD

1. In a food processor, pulse the cucumbers until finely chopped but not pureed. Drain off any liquid and transfer to a medium bowl.
2. Add the yogurt, garlic, lemon juice, dill, and protein powder to the cucumbers. Season with salt to taste and mix well.
3. Serve as a dip or as a great sauce for a protein.

PER SERVING
63 calories / 3g fat / 6g protein
9g carbohydrates / 3g fiber

PROTEIN PIZZA CRUST

MAKES 4 SERVINGS

———————————

I've baked nutrition right into this pizza crust—baby spinach, a supergreen, is incorporated into the dough! I left it open for you to top the crust with anything you desire, but I suggest sticking to veggies, nondairy cheese, and turkey sausage.

PREP TIME: 5 MINUTES
COOK TIME: 15 MINUTES

INGREDIENTS

2   cups baby spinach
1   scoop Rocco's Protein Baking Mix or
    your favorite baking mix (such as Bob's
    Red Mill)
    Pinch of salt
¼   cup liquid egg whites
1   egg

METHOD

1. Preheat the oven to 400°F. Line a rimmed baking sheet with a silicone baking mat or use an ovenproof nonstick pan.
2. In a food processor, combine the spinach, protein baking mix, and salt and pulse until it is almost the texture of sand, 8 to 10 times. With the processor running, pour in the liquid egg whites and whole egg.
3. Transfer the dough to the baking sheet and bake until the center of the pizza crust is set, 12 to 15 minutes.

Tip: Put any ingredients you would like on your crust and broil for a few minutes to warm through—and melt any cheese.

PER SERVING
62 calories / 1g fat / 9g protein
3g carbohydrates / 3g fiber

5/5/2018
2 eggs
Spinach
Cavendish Scoop
Salt

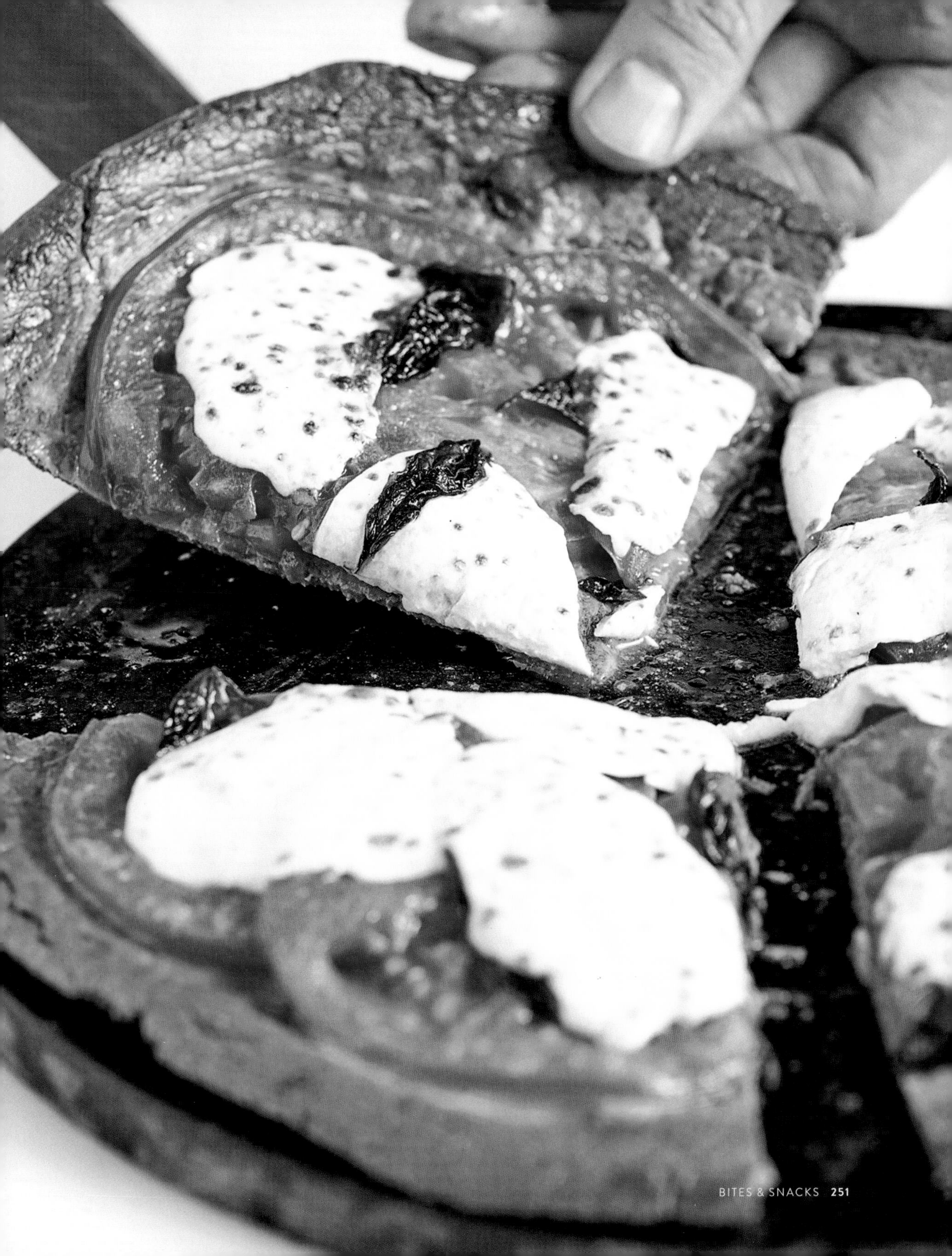

DEVILED EGGS

MAKES 4 SERVINGS

I've scarfed down many deviled eggs in my day, and I love the old-fashioned kind—you know, with mayonnaise and yellow mustard. In my lightened up version, I've used coconut yogurt to replace the mayonnaise and dispensed with the mustard altogether. When I brought a batch of these to a party recently, they were gone in minutes!

PREP TIME: 10 MINUTES
COOK TIME: 15 MINUTES

INGREDIENTS

4   eggs
½   teaspoon smoked paprika, plus more for sprinkling
1   tablespoon chopped Italian flat parsley
1   teaspoon lemon juice
2   tablespoons unsweetened nondairy coconut yogurt (such as So Delicious)
    Cayenne pepper

METHOD

1. Set up a bowl of ice and water. Place the eggs in a small pot and add water to just cover. Bring the water to a boil and cook the eggs for precisely 8 minutes. Drain and transfer to the ice bath to cool. Peel when they are cool enough to handle.

2. Halve the eggs lengthwise. Scoop the yolks into a small bowl and set the whites aside.

3. Add the smoked paprika, parsley, lemon juice, yogurt, and cayenne to taste to the egg yolks and mix to combine. Spoon the mixture into the reserved egg whites and sprinkle with smoked paprika. Serve immediately.

Tip: Add a dash of salt to the water before you cook the eggs to make peeling them easier!

PER SERVING
77 calories / 5g fat / 6g protein
1g carbohydrate / <1g fiber

AVOCADO PIMENTÓN DIP

MAKES 4 SERVINGS

PREP TIME: 10 MINUTES

INGREDIENTS

2 avocados
  Juice of 2 limes
½ teaspoon pimentón
½ diced shallot
  Salt and pepper

METHOD

1. Scoop the insides of the avocados into a zip-top bag. Add the lime juice and pimentón. Get as much air out as possible and close the bag.
2. Press the bagged avocados with your hands or a rolling pin until the avocado is smashed into small pieces and well mixed with the lime juice and pimentón.
3. Cut a hole in the corner of the bag and squeeze the avocado into a small bowl. Mix in the shallot, season with salt and pepper, and serve.

PER SERVING
121 calories / 10g fat / 1g protein
8g carbohydrates / 5g fiber

EGGPLANT WALNUT DIP

MAKES 4 SERVINGS

PREP TIME: 5 MINUTES
COOK TIME: 10 MINUTES

INGREDIENTS

1   large eggplant
¼   cup raw walnuts
1   tablespoon garlic oil
1   tablespoon apple cider vinegar
1   teaspoon ground ginger

METHOD

1. Pierce the eggplant with a paring knife and place it on a microwave-safe dish. Microwave until it softens, 10 to 12 minutes, depending on the size of your eggplant.
2. Scoop the eggplant flesh into a food processor. Add the walnuts, garlic oil, vinegar, and ginger and puree until smooth.

PER SERVING

117 calories / 8g fat / 3g protein
11g carbohydrates / 6g fiber

CHIPOTLE BLACK BEAN DIP

MAKES 4 SERVINGS

PREP TIME: 15 MINUTES

INGREDIENTS

2   cups canned black beans,
    drained and rinsed
3   chipotle peppers in adobo sauce
    Juice of 2 limes
2   tablespoons water

METHOD

In a food processor, combine the beans
chipotles, lime juice, and water and blend
until fairly smooth, about 1 minute. There
should still be a bit of texture to the beans.

PER SERVING
100 calories / <1g fat / 4g protein
13g carbohydrates / 4g fiber

SWEET PEA HUMMUS

MAKES 4 SERVINGS

Hummus is traditionally made with chickpeas, but you won't believe how wonderful it tastes made with peas. The flavor is a bit more delicate, but luscious. This is a dish that can be whipped up in seconds. I suggest serving it with crudités or using it as a sandwich spread.

PREP TIME: 5 MINUTES

INGREDIENTS

1   cup frozen peas, thawed
2   tablespoons tahini
1   tablespoon extra-virgin olive oil
1   clove garlic
2   tablespoons lemon juice
2   tablespoons water

METHOD

In a food processor, combine the peas, tahini, olive oil, garlic, lemon juice, and water and pulse 5 times to get the mixture going. Then puree until smooth, about 1 minute. Use immediately or store tightly sealed in the refrigerator for up to 1 week.

PER SERVING
97 calories / 8g fat / 2g protein
2g carbohydrates / <1g fiber

SMOKY KALE CHIPS

MAKES 1 SERVING

PREP TIME: 2 MINUTES
COOK TIME: 2 MINUTES

INGREDIENTS

1   ounce baby kale
    Olive oil (in a spray bottle)
    Pinch of smoked paprika

METHOD

1. Place the kale in a single layer on a microwave-safe plate lined with a paper towel.
2. Coat with 1 spray of oil from the spray bottle held 18 inches from the plate. Sprinkle with the smoked paprika.
3. Microwave on 70 percent power for 45 seconds. Then microwave on high for another 30 seconds. Serve immediately.

Tip: If you don't have an olive oil spray bottle, a spritz of olive oil or coconut oil cooking spray works just as well.

PER SERVING
25 calories / 1g fat / <1g protein
3g carbohydrates / <1g fiber

NORI ROLLS WITH MANGO RED CHILE SAUCE

MAKES 2 SERVINGS

In the mood for sushi but don't feel like going out or spending the money on expensive rolls? This sweet-and-savory vegetarian nori roll recipe comes together quickly and will satisfy your sushi cravings.

PREP TIME: 20 MINUTES

INGREDIENTS

1   cup diced mango
    Red chile flakes
¼   cup water
1   tablespoon lime juice
1   cup julienned carrots (shaved with the julienne teeth on a mandoline)
½   English (seedless) cucumber, julienned on a mandoline
4   nori sheets

METHOD

1. In a blender, combine the mango, chile flakes, water, and lime juice and puree until smooth, about 60 seconds.
2. Lay the carrots and cucumber out onto the nori sheets and roll like sushi or a pinwheel. Serve with the mango dipping sauce on the side.

PER SERVING
49 calories / <1g fat / 2g protein
13g carbohydrates / 2g fiber

SALT AND BATTERY POPCORN

MAKES 4 SERVINGS

PREP TIME: 5 MINUTES

INGREDIENTS

¼ cup unpopped popcorn kernels
    Cooking spray
1½ teaspoons malt vinegar powder
½ teaspoon sea salt

METHOD

1. Place the popcorn kernels in an air-pop popcorn machine. Turn the machine on and pop the corn.
2. Spray the popped corn lightly with cooking spray. Toss with the malt vinegar powder and sea salt.

PER SERVING
40 calories / <1g fat / 1g protein
10g carbohydrates / 2g fiber

CABBAGE SLAW

MAKES 4 SERVINGS

I love experimenting with conflicting flavors so I've jazzed this slaw up with a secret ingredient: grated radish. It really gives the slaw a zing that plays beautifully off the sweetness of the other ingredients. I should confess though, that radish isn't such a secret ingredient; Asian slaws feature it all the time.

PREP TIME: 15 MINUTES

INGREDIENTS

- 4 cups shredded cabbage
- 1½ cups peeled grated carrots (grated on the large holes of a box grater)
- ¾ cup grated radish (grated on the large holes of a box grater)
- ¼ cup white wine vinegar
- ½ cup unsweetened nondairy coconut yogurt (such as So Delicious)
- 4 packets Monk Fruit in the Raw
  Salt and pepper

METHOD

In a large bowl, combine the cabbage, carrots, radish, vinegar, yogurt, monk fruit, and salt and pepper to taste and toss well to combine. Leftovers can be stored tightly sealed in the refrigerator for a few days.

PER SERVING
49 calories / 1g fat / 2g protein
10g carbohydrates / 3g fiber

CRISPY RAS EL HANOUT CAULIFLOWER

MAKES 4 SERVINGS

PREP TIME: 10 MINUTES
COOK TIME: 30 MINUTES

INGREDIENTS

2   heads cauliflower, cut into bite-size florets
2   tablespoons extra-virgin olive oil
2   teaspoons ras el hanout

METHOD

1. Preheat the oven to 375°F. Line a baking sheet with parchment paper.
2. Place the cauliflower into a large bowl. Sprinkle with the olive oil and ras el hanout and toss to coat.
3. Arrange the cauliflower on the lined baking sheet and bake until the insides are tender and the outsides are very crisp, about 30 minutes.

Tip: This recipe makes a great lunch with a fried egg on top for an extra 80 calories.

PER SERVING
130 calories / 7g fat / 5g protein
15g carbohydrates / 7g fiber

PEOPLE PUPPY CHOW

MAKES 4 SERVINGS

PREP TIME: 10 MINUTES

INGREDIENTS

½ cup puffed rice cereal
2 tablespoons unsweetened almond butter
1 teaspoon unsweetened cocoa powder
¼ cup raw almonds, roughly chopped
2 tablespoons cacao nibs
4 packets Monk Fruit in the Raw

METHOD

1. In a large bowl, use your hands to combine the puffed rice, almond butter, and cocoa powder.
2. Add the almonds and cacao nibs to the bowl and mix well.
3. Cover the cereal mix with monk fruit and toss to coat and keep from sticking together.

PER SERVING
109 calories / 9g fat / 3g protein
6g carbohydrates / 2g fiber

PUMPKIN SPICE TRAIL MIX

MAKES 4 SERVINGS

PREP TIME: 10 MINUTES

INGREDIENTS

¼ cup raw whole almonds

¼ cup raw pumpkin seeds

¼ cup freeze-dried cranberries

¼ cup rolled oats

¼ teaspoon extra-virgin olive oil

½ teaspoon pumpkin pie spice

METHOD

In a small bowl, combine the almonds, pumpkin seeds, cranberries, oats, olive oil, and pumpkin pie spice and toss to mix well.

PER SERVING

110 calories / 8g fat / 5g protein
7g carbohydrates / 3g fiber

ALMOND POPCORN TRAIL MIX

MAKES 4 SERVINGS

PREP TIME: 10 MINUTES

INGREDIENTS

1 cup air-popped popcorn

¼ cup raw whole almonds

2 tablespoons stevia-sweetened chocolate chips (such as Lily's)

¼ cup unsweetened coconut flakes

METHOD

In a small bowl, combine the popcorn, almonds, chocolate chips, and coconut flakes and toss well.

PER SERVING

91 calories / 8g fat / 3g protein
8g carbohydrates / 4g fiber

SWEET AND SPICY NUT MIX

MAKES 4 SERVINGS

PREP TIME: 5 MINUTES
COOK TIME: 10 MINUTES

INGREDIENTS

½ brown rice cake

¼ cup raw cashews

¼ cup raw almonds

1 teaspoon hemp hearts

1 tablespoon egg whites

½ teaspoon *yuzu kosho*

1 teaspoon reduced-sodium tamari

METHOD

1. Preheat the oven to 325°F. Line a baking sheet with parchment paper.
2. Break the rice cake apart with your fingers.
3. In a medium bowl, combine the rice cake, cashews, almonds, hemp hearts, egg whites, *yuzu kosho*, and tamari and toss to coat well.
4. Spread on the lined baking sheet and bake until set, about 10 minutes. Let cool, then break into bite-size pieces.

Tip: If you can't find *yuzu kosho* in stores, it is readily available online.

PER SERVING
112 calories / 8g fat / 5g protein
<1g carbohydrate / 2g fiber

TRAIL OF LIFE MIX

MAKES 4 SERVINGS

PREP TIME: 10 MINUTES

INGREDIENTS

½   brown rice cake

¼   cup whole raw almonds

¼   cup raw pumpkin seeds

2   tablespoons dried golden berries

2   tablespoons dried mulberries

1   tablespoon goji berries

1   tablespoon stevia-sweetened dark
    chocolate chips (such as Lily's)
    Cayenne pepper

METHOD

Break the rice cake apart with your fingers and place it in a small bowl. Add the almonds, pumpkin seeds, golden berries, mulberries, goji berries, chocolate chips, and cayenne (as much as you can take!) and toss to combine.

PER SERVING
128 calories / 8g fat / 5g protein
12g carbohydrates / 4g fiber

CHUNKY MONKEY TRAIL MIX

MAKES 4 SERVINGS

PREP TIME: 10 MINUTES

INGREDIENTS

¼   cup raw whole walnuts

¼   cup raw pistachios

2   tablespoons cacao nibs

2   tablespoons stevia-sweetened chocolate chips (such as Lily's)

½   brown rice cake

½   teaspoon banana extract

METHOD

1. In a small bowl, combine the walnuts, pistachios, cacao nibs, chocolate chips, and rice cake and toss well to mix.
2. Pour the banana extract on top of the mixture and mix once more.
3. Allow to sit out for a few minutes before serving so the alcohol can evaporate from the banana extract.

PER SERVING

130 calories / 11g fat / 3g protein
10g carbohydrates / 3g fiber

BLOODY MARY
TRAIL MIX

MAKES 4 SERVINGS

_____

PREP TIME: 10 MINUTES

INGREDIENTS

4   ounces brown rice cakes
2   ounces raw whole almonds
2   ounces raw whole cashews
1   ounce goji berries
1   ounce dried apricots, finely diced
1   teaspoon Worcestershire sauce
2   dashes Tabasco sauce

METHOD

Crumble the rice cakes with your hands into a bowl. Add the almonds, cashews, goji berries, apricots, Worcestershire sauce, and Tabasco and mix with your hands.

Tip: Add a bit more Tabasco if you can take the heat.

PER SERVING
131 calories / 8g fat / 4g protein
13g carbohydrates / 3g fiber

THANKSGIVING TRAIL MIX

MAKES 4 SERVINGS

PREP TIME: 10 MINUTES

INGREDIENTS

¼   cup raw pecans

¼   cup raw cashews

¼   cup freeze-dried cranberries

½   brown rice cake, crumbled

¼   teaspoon extra-virgin olive oil

½   teaspoon poultry seasoning
    Salt and pepper

METHOD

In a small bowl, combine the nuts, cranberries, rice cake, olive oil, poultry seasoning, and salt and pepper to taste and toss well to combine.

PER SERVING
88 calories / 7g fat / 2g protein
5g carbohydrates / 2g fiber

CAJUN PECAN TRAIL MIX

PREP TIME: 10 MINUTES

INGREDIENTS

- ¼ cup plus 2 tablespoons raw whole cashews
- 2 tablespoons raw whole pecans
- ¼ cup dried golden berries
- ½ cup puffed rice cereal
- 2 tablespoons goji berries
- ¼ teaspoon extra-virgin olive oil
  Pinch of cayenne pepper

METHOD

In a small bowl, combine the nuts, golden berries, puffed rice, and goji berries and toss to mix. Add the olive oil and cayenne and toss again.

PER SERVING
124 calories / 8g fat / 3g protein
8g carbohydrates / 2g fiber

COCOA-NUTTY
TRAIL MIX

MAKES 4 SERVINGS

PREP TIME: 5 MINUTES

INGREDIENTS

¼   cup raw cashews

¼   cup raw pistachios

2   tablespoons unsweetened coconut chips

2   tablespoons goji berries

1   tablespoon stevia-sweetened chocolate chips (such as Lily's)

¼   cup puffed rice cereal

3   packets Monk Fruit in the Raw

1   teaspoon unsweetened cocoa powder

METHOD

In a small bowl, combine the nuts, coconut chips, goji berries, chocolate chips, and puffed rice. Sprinkle the monk fruit and cocoa powder on top and toss to mix.

PER SERVING
117 calories / 8.5g fat
31g carbohydrates / 11g fiber

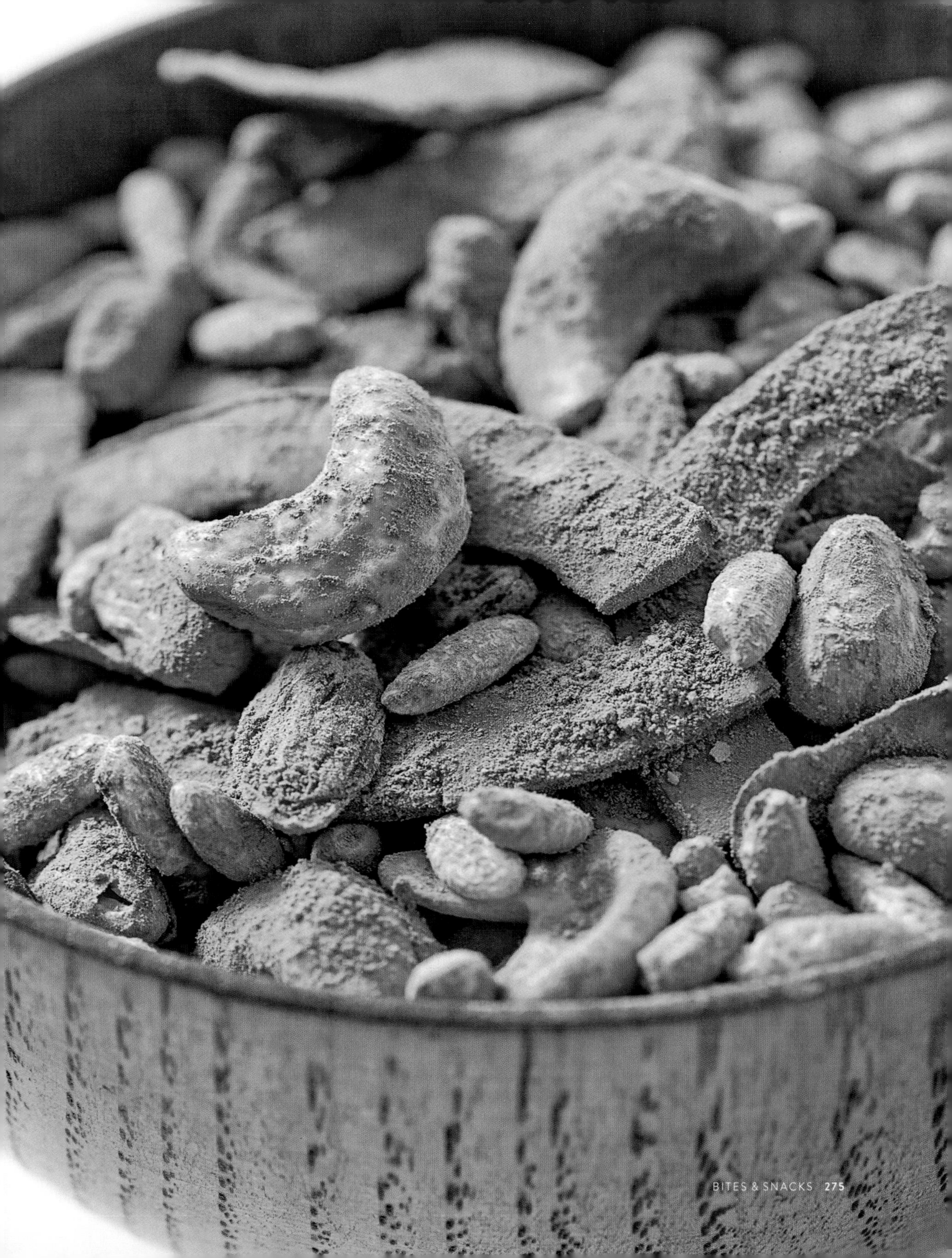

BLACK FOREST TRAIL MIX

MAKES 4 SERVINGS

PREP TIME: 5 MINUTES

INGREDIENTS

¼ cup raw cashews

¼ cup raw hazelnuts

2 tablespoons cacao nibs

3 tablespoons unsweetened dried cherries (such as Country Spoon)

½ brown rice cake, crumbled

METHOD

In a small bowl, combine the nuts, cacao nibs, cherries, and rice cake and mix well.

PER SERVING

128 calories / 9g fat / 3g protein

9g carbohydrates / 2g fiber

MOUNT KATAHDIN KRUNCH

MAKES 4 SERVINGS

PREP TIME: 5 MINUTES
COOK TIME: 10 MINUTES

INGREDIENTS

½ brown rice cake, crumbled

½ cup unsweetened dried blueberries

¼ cup raw pumpkin seeds

¼ cup raw walnuts

1 tablespoon egg white

½ teaspoon vanilla extract

METHOD

1. Preheat the oven to 325°F. Line a baking sheet with parchment paper.

2. In a small bowl, combine the rice cake, blueberries, pumpkin seeds, walnuts, egg white, and vanilla and mix well.

3. Spread on the lined baking sheet and bake until the mixture is crispy, about 10 minutes.

4. Let cool, then break into large chunks.

PER SERVING
108 calories / 8g fat / 4g protein
7g carbohydrates / 2g fiber

CHAPTER 10

Avocado Dishes

AVOCADO AND SHRIMP SALAD

MAKES 4 SERVINGS

PREP TIME: 10 MINUTES
COOK TIME: 5 MINUTES

INGREDIENTS

½   pound shrimp, heads and tails removed
½   cup diced celery
¼   cup unsweetened nondairy coconut
     yogurt (such as So Delicious)
1   tablespoon lemon juice
     Tabasco sauce
     Salt and pepper
2   avocados

METHOD

1. Set up a bowl of ice and water. Bring a small pot of water to a boil. Add the shrimp and cook until tender, but not like rubber, about 3 minutes. Remove to the ice bath, then drain.

2. Cut the shrimp into bite-size pieces and place in a small bowl. Add the celery, yogurt, lemon juice, Tabasco to taste, and salt and pepper to taste. Mix well.

3. Halve and pit the avocados. Fill the centers with the shrimp salad.

PER SERVING
173 calories / 11g fat / 13g protein
7g carbohydrates / 5g fiber

AVOCADO AND ALMOND RICOTTA

MAKES 4 SERVINGS

PREP TIME: 15 MINUTES
SOAK TIME: 30 MINUTES

INGREDIENTS

½ cup raw almonds
2 tablespoons lemon juice
½ cup basil leaves, torn
2 tablespoons grated Parmesan cheese
Salt and pepper
2 avocados

METHOD

1. Bring a small pot of water to a boil. Place the almonds in a small heatproof container and pour the boiling water over them. Set aside for 30 minutes to allow them to soften.

2. Reserving the soaking water, drain the almonds, and transfer to a blender. Add the lemon juice, basil, Parmesan, and salt and pepper to taste. Puree until the mixture achieves the texture of ricotta, about 1 minute. If the mixture is dry, add some of the soaking liquid 1 tablespoon at a time to hydrate and loosen.

3. Halve and pit the avocados. Scoop the almond ricotta into the centers.

PER SERVING
201 calories / 17g fat / 5g protein
8g carbohydrates / 6g fiber

AVOCADO KIMCHI

MAKES 4 SERVINGS

PREP TIME: 5 MINUTES

INGREDIENTS

2   avocados

1   cup kimchi (such as Ozuké), chopped

METHOD

Halve and pit the avocados. Top with the chopped kimchi.

Tip: Be sure to check the label on the kimchi. Many have added sugars—avoid those!

PER SERVING
107 calories / 9g fat / 1g protein
6g carbohydrates / 4g fiber

DEVILED AVOCADO

MAKES 4 SERVINGS

PREP TIME: 10 MINUTES

INGREDIENTS

2 avocados

3 tablespoons finely diced shallot

2 tablespoons lime juice

½ teaspoon paprika

½ teaspoon smoked paprika

Cayenne pepper

METHOD

1. Scoop the flesh of the avocados into a medium bowl. Save the skins for later.

2. Add the shallot, lime juice, both paprikas, and cayenne to taste and mash with a fork until smooth. Scoop into the avocado skins and serve.

PER SERVING

111 calories / 10g fat / 2g protein

7g carbohydrates / 5g fiber

AVOCADO FURIKAKE

MAKES 4 SERVINGS

PREP TIME: 10 MINUTES

INGREDIENTS

2   tablespoons reduced-sodium tamari

2   tablespoons lemon juice

2   avocados

4   tablespoons furikake seasoning (such as
    Eden Foods Eden Shake)

METHOD

1. In a small bowl, mix the tamari and lemon
   juice together.

2. Halve and pit the avocados. Score
   the flesh with a paring knife. Pour
   1 tablespoon of the tamari mixture on
   each half. Shake 1 tablespoon of the
   furikake on top of each.

PER SERVING
122 calories / 9g fat / 2g protein
8g carbohydrates / 6g fiber

AVOCADO AND CUCUMBER RAITA

MAKES 4 SERVINGS

PREP TIME: 15 MINUTES

INGREDIENTS

1   cup finely chopped cucumber

½   cup unsweetened nondairy coconut
    yogurt (such as So Delicious)

2   tablespoons chopped mint

¼   teaspoon ground cumin
    Salt and pepper

1   clove garlic

2   avocados

METHOD

1. In a small bowl, mix together the cucumber, yogurt, mint, cumin, and salt and pepper to taste.
2. Finely grate the garlic into the bowl and mix all ingredients well.
3. Halve and pit the avocados. Spoon the raita into the center of the avocados and serve.

Tip: Try cilantro in the raita instead of the mint.

PER SERVING
124 calories / 10g fat / 1g protein
8g carbohydrates / 4g fiber

AVOCADO, SALUMI, AND PICKLES

MAKES 4 SERVINGS

PREP TIME: 20 MINUTES
COOK TIME: 5 MINUTES

INGREDIENTS

½   cup cucumber slices, ⅛ inch thick
½   cup apple cider vinegar
½   cup water
1   teaspoon fennel seeds
4   packets Monk Fruit in the Raw
    Salt and pepper
2   avocados
1   tablespoon lime juice
8   very thin slices bresaola

METHOD

1. Place the cucumbers in a small heatproof bowl.
2. In a small saucepan, combine the vinegar, water, fennel seeds, monk fruit, and salt and pepper to taste and bring just to a boil. Pour over the cucumbers and set aside for 10 minutes.
3. Mash the avocados and lime juice together.
4. Spoon the avocado mixture onto the bresaola and top with a few cucumber pickle slices. Roll into a cylinder or eat as you would a taco.

PER SERVING
137 calories / 10g fat / 4g protein
11g carbohydrates / 4g fiber

AVOCADO AND CELERY ROOT SALAD

MAKES 4 SERVINGS

PREP TIME: 20 MINUTES

INGREDIENTS

2 cups grated celery root (grated on the large holes of a box grater)
  Salt
4 teaspoons Dijon mustard
¼ cup unsweetened nondairy coconut yogurt (such as So Delicious)
¼ cup chopped Italian flat parsley
  Pepper
2 avocados

METHOD

1. Place the celery root in a colander, lightly salt it, and set aside for 10 minutes to allow to soften.
2. Squeeze the moisture out of the celery root with your hands and transfer to a bowl. Add the mustard, yogurt, and parsley and season with pepper.
3. Halve and pit the avocados. Fill with the celery root salad.

PER SERVING
137 calories / 10g fat / 2g protein
11g carbohydrates / 5g fiber

AVOCADO SALSA VERDE

MAKES 4 SERVINGS

PREP TIME: 10 MINUTES

INGREDIENTS

2   cups diced tomatillos

1   tablespoon minced jalapeño
    (seeded and deribbed)

¼   cup chopped cilantro

2   tablespoons lime juice

1   tablespoon extra-virgin olive oil
    Salt and pepper

2   avocados

METHOD

1. In a small bowl, combine the tomatillos,
   jalapeño, cilantro, lime juice, olive oil, and
   salt and pepper to taste and mix well.

2. Halve and pit the avocados. Spoon the
   salsa into the centers.

PER SERVING

150 calories / 13g fat / 2g protein
8g carbohydrates / 5g fiber

AVOCADO AND SALMON SALAD

MAKES 4 SERVINGS

———————————————

PREP TIME: 10 MINUTES

INGREDIENTS

2   cans (5 ounces each) water-packed salmon, drained
¼   cup unsweetened nondairy coconut yogurt (such as So Delicious)
2   teaspoons apple cider vinegar
3   tablespoons chopped Italian flat parsley
    Salt and pepper
2   avocados

METHOD

1. In a large bowl, combine the salmon, yogurt, vinegar, parsley, and salt and pepper to taste and mix well.
2. Halve and pit the avocados. Fill the centers with the salmon salad.

PER SERVING
171 calories / 11g fat / 13g protein
6g carbohydrates / 4g fiber

AVOCADO TOMATO BALSAMIC

MAKES 4 SERVINGS

This dish is the ultimate avocado salad. Avocados are cool because when you remove the pit, what's left is a nice little hole into which you can stuff other veggies. Here I've done that with tomatoes and basil, and drizzled it with balsamic vinegar.

PREP TIME: 10 MINUTES

INGREDIENTS

1½ cups diced tomatoes

¼ cup basil leaves, torn into bite-size pieces

Salt and pepper

2 avocados

4 teaspoons balsamic vinegar

METHOD

1. In a small bowl, toss together the tomatoes, basil, and salt and pepper to taste.
2. Halve and pit the avocados and fill with the tomato mixture. Season with salt and pepper. Drizzle the balsamic vinegar on top of everything.

PER SERVING

123 calories / 10g fat / 2g protein
10g carbohydrates / 5g fiber

CAPRESE AVOCADO TOAST

MAKES 4 SERVINGS

———————————

PREP TIME: 10 MINUTES

INGREDIENTS

2   gluten-free sprouted English muffins (such as Food for Life)
1   avocado
4   slices tomato (¼ inch thick)
½   cup torn basil

METHOD

1. Split the English muffins and toast.
2. Place the avocado in a small bowl and mash with a fork until it becomes the consistency of butter. Spread over the English muffins.
3. Top each with a slice of tomato and some of the torn basil.

Tip: Add a drizzle of balsamic vinegar for extra flavor.

PER SERVING
168 calories / 5g fat / 2g protein
28g carbohydrates / 5g fiber

STRAWBERRY AVOCADO TOAST

MAKES 4 SERVINGS

PREP TIME: 10 MINUTES
COOK TIME: 5 MINUTES

INGREDIENTS

⅔ cup buckwheat flour
1 teaspoon baking powder
   Pinch of salt
2 eggs
¼ cup unsweetened coconut milk beverage, (such as So Delicious)
2 avocados
1 tablespoon lime juice
½ cup sliced strawberries

METHOD

1. Coat two coffee mugs with cooking spray.
2. In a small bowl, combine the buckwheat flour, baking powder, salt, eggs, and coconut milk and stir well with a fork to combine.
3. Divide the batter evenly among the coffee mugs and microwave until a toothpick inserted in the bread comes out clean, about 90 seconds.
4. Turn the breads out. Slice into 8 pieces, 4 per loaf, and toast.
5. Mash the avocados and lime juice together with a fork and spread it over the toasted bread. Top with the strawberries.

PER SERVING
214 calories / 13g fat / 7g protein
21g carbohydrates / 7g fiber

CORN AND CHIMICHURRI AVOCADO TOAST

MAKES 4 SERVINGS

PREP TIME: 15 MINUTES

INGREDIENTS

½ cup chopped Italian flat parsley

1 clove garlic

2 tablespoons red wine vinegar

½ jalapeño, chopped

1 tablespoon extra-virgin olive oil

2 gluten-free sprouted English muffins (such as Food for Life)

1 avocado

½ cup freeze-dried corn

Salt and pepper

METHOD

1. In a food processor, combine the parsley, garlic, vinegar, jalapeño, and olive oil and puree briefly, about 15 seconds, just to break up the parsley and garlic. Set the chimichurri aside.

2. Split the English muffins and toast them.

3. Mash the avocado and spread it on each half. Sprinkle with the corn and press to get it to adhere to the avocado. Season with salt and pepper and drizzle the chimichurri on top.

PER SERVING

226 calories / 9g fat / 3g protein
34g carbohydrates / 5g fiber

DUKKAH AVOCADO TOAST

MAKES 4 SERVINGS

PREP TIME: 10 MINUTES

INGREDIENTS

¼ cup raw almonds

1 tablespoon sesame seeds

½ teaspoon ground coriander

¼ teaspoon ground cumin
   Salt and pepper

2 gluten-free sprouted English muffins
   (such as Food for Life)

1 avocado

METHOD

1. In a blender, pulse the almonds until finely ground, about 8 times. Transfer to a small bowl.

2. Add the sesame seeds, coriander, cumin, and salt and pepper to taste. Toss well to mix. Set aside. (This is *dukkah*—a traditional Egyptian condiment.)

3. Split the English muffins and toast them.

4. Mash the avocado with a fork and spread it on the English muffins. Top with the *dukkah* and season with salt and pepper.

PER SERVING
220 calories / 10g fat / 4g protein
29g carbohydrates / 6g fiber

NON-GRINGO AVOCADO TOAST

MAKES 4 SERVINGS

—————

PREP TIME: 15 MINUTES
COOK TIME: 5 MINUTES

INGREDIENTS

⅔ cup almond meal/flour

1 teaspoon baking powder
Salt

2 eggs

¼ cup unsweetened coconut milk beverage (such as So Delicious)

2 avocados

½ cup jarred salsa (such as Brad's Organic)
Pepper

METHOD

1. Coat a microwave-safe glass with cooking spray.

2. In a small bowl, combine the almond meal, baking powder, a pinch of salt, the eggs, and coconut milk with a fork. Pour into the glass and microwave until a toothpick inserted into the center of the bread comes out clean, about 90 seconds.

3. Remove from the glass. Slice into 8 pieces and toast them.

4. Mash the avocados with a fork. Spread onto the toast and top with the salsa. Season with salt and pepper.

Tip: Top with cilantro to enliven the flavor even more.

PER SERVING
256 calories / 21g fat / 8g protein
11g carbohydrates / 6g fiber

SMOKED SALMON AVOCADO TOAST

MAKES 4 SERVINGS

PREP TIME: 10 MINUTES
COOK TIME: 2 MINUTES

INGREDIENTS

⅔ cup buckwheat flour

1 teaspoon baking powder
   Pinch of salt

2 eggs

2 avocados

2 tablespoons lemon juice

8 ounces smoked salmon

1 tablespoon chopped chives

METHOD

1. Coat two coffee mugs with cooking spray.

2. In a small bowl, combine the buckwheat flour, baking powder, salt, and eggs with a fork.

3. Divide the mixture evenly between the mugs and microwave until a toothpick inserted in a bread comes out clean, about 90 seconds. Turn the bread out. Slice into 8 rounds total.

4. Mash together the avocados and lemon juice, leaving some chunks of avocado. Spread on the toast rounds.

5. Top the avocado with the salmon and chives.

PER SERVING
276 calories / 15g fat / 20g protein
20g carbohydrates / 7g fiber

CHAPTER 11

Sides & Sauces

HARD-ROASTED BROCCOLI WITH NUTS AND LEMON

MAKES 4 SERVINGS

PREP TIME: 5 MINUTES
COOK TIME: 20 MINUTES

INGREDIENTS

1½ pounds broccoli florets
2   tablespoons extra-virgin olive oil
     Salt and pepper
1   teaspoon grated lemon zest
½   teaspoon lemon juice
¼   cup raw almonds, roughly chopped

METHOD

1. Preheat the oven to 400°F. Line a baking sheet with parchment paper.
2. In a large bowl, toss the broccoli florets with the olive oil. Season with salt and pepper.
3. Place on the lined baking sheet and bake until crispy on the outside yet tender on the inside, about 20 minutes.
4. Transfer the broccoli to a bowl and toss with the lemon zest, lemon juice, and almonds.

PER SERVING
163 calories / 11g fat / 6g protein
30g carbohydrates / 5g fiber

BEET, CARROT, AND KALE SLAW

MAKES 4 SERVINGS

PREP TIME: 15 MINUTES

INGREDIENTS

4   cups peeled grated golden beets (grated on the large holes of a box grater)
2   cups peeled grated carrots (grated on the large holes of a box grater)
3   cups chopped kale
½   cup unsweetened nondairy coconut yogurt (such as So Delicious)
3   tablespoons lemon juice
1   tablespoon Dijon mustard
    Salt and pepper

METHOD

In a large bowl, mix together the beets, carrots, kale, yogurt, lemon juice, and mustard. Season with salt and pepper. Toss well to combine.

PER SERVING
87 calories / 1g fat / 3g protein
18g carbohydrates / 4g fiber

STUFFED BELL PEPPERS

MAKES 4 SERVINGS

With their bright color and unusual shape, stuffed peppers showcase a stunning presentation for any course. Bell peppers come in different colors. If you choose red, you'll have a pepper that is sweeter and milder than a green bell pepper, with more beta-carotene and vitamin C, too. This recipe is gluten-free and vegan-friendly.

PREP TIME: 15 MINUTES

PER SERVING
88 calories / 1g fat / 4g protein
20g carbohydrates / 6g fiber

INGREDIENTS

4   small bell peppers
2   medium carrots, chopped
2   medium zucchini, chopped
1   cup chopped tomatoes
1   teaspoon ground coriander
    Salt and pepper
3   tablespoons chopped chives

METHOD

1. Cut the tops off the bell peppers and remove the seeds and as much of the ribs as you can. Set aside.

2. In a food processor, combine the carrots, zucchini, tomatoes, and coriander and pulse 7 to 10 times to form a mixture roughly the consistency of ground meat. Season with salt and pepper. Spoon into the peppers, top with the chives, and serve.

ROASTED CORN

MAKES 4 SERVINGS

PREP TIME: 5 MINUTES
COOK TIME: 25 MINUTES

INGREDIENTS

2 medium ears husked corn
    (about 6 inches each)

1 tablespoon extra-virgin olive oil

2 teaspoons rosemary leaves
    Salt and pepper

METHOD

1. Preheat the oven to 400°F.
2. Place each ear of corn onto a piece of foil. Brush each with olive oil and sprinkle with the rosemary and salt and pepper to taste. Wrap tightly and transfer to a baking sheet. Roast until the kernels are tender, about 20 minutes.
3. Leave the corn wrapped in the foil until time to serve, then peel and cut each ear in half.

PER SERVING

76 calories / 4g fat / 2g protein
10g carbohydrates / 1g fiber

BBQ SPAGHETTI SQUASH

MAKES 4 SERVINGS

When baked, spaghetti squash can be easily separated into strands that sort of resemble spaghetti—hence the name. This veggie is a perfect way to create pasta-like meals minus the carbs and calories. In this recipe, you get to top it with a rich barbecue sauce that pairs well with this mild, sweet vegetable.

PREP TIME: 10 MINUTES
COOK TIME: 15 MINUTES

INGREDIENTS

1   medium spaghetti squash, halved and seeded

¼   cup tomato paste

¼   cup unsweetened ketchup

½   teaspoon chili powder

½   teaspoon garlic powder

1   teaspoon Worcestershire sauce

¼   cup water

1   packet Monk Fruit in the Raw
    Salt and pepper

METHOD

1. Place the spaghetti squash on a large microwave-safe dish. Add enough water to coat the bottom of the dish and cover tightly with microwaveable wrap. Microwave until the squash is tender, 12 to 15 minutes.

2. Meanwhile, in a small bowl, mix together the tomato paste, ketchup, chili powder, garlic powder, Worcestershire sauce, water, and monk fruit. Season with salt and pepper.

3. Remove the squash from the microwave. When cool enough to handle, use a fork to separate the strands of squash from one another, pulling them into a large microwave-safe bowl. Pour the sauce on top of the squash and toss to coat. Microwave 2 to 3 minutes longer to finish cooking the squash.

PER SERVING
118 calories / 2g fat / 3g protein
25g carbohydrates / 7g fiber

MUSHROOM BRUSCHETTA

MAKES 4 SERVINGS

Often served as an appetizer, bruschetta is the original Italian garlic bread. It can be topped with just about anything—tomatoes, sautéed greens, herbs, olives, and more. In this recipe, I've chosen earthy, nutty cremini mushrooms paired with garlic and thyme.

PREP TIME: 10 MINUTES
COOK TIME: 10 MINUTES

INGREDIENTS

1   pound cremini mushrooms
2   cloves garlic
2   teaspoons thyme leaves
    Salt and pepper
4   slices gluten-free bread
2   tablespoons chopped Italian flat parsley

METHOD

1. Cut the mushrooms into large pieces.
2. Heat a pan over high heat until very hot, about 3 minutes. Add the mushrooms with 1 clove of the garlic and the thyme. Cook, tossing the mushrooms occasionally and letting them brown, about 10 minutes. Season with salt and pepper and remove from the heat.
3. Lightly toast the gluten-free bread.
4. Rub the toast with the remaining garlic clove. Divide the mushrooms evenly among the toasts and top with the parsley.

Tip: For even more flavor, add a bit of shaved Parmesan cheese.

PER SERVING
78 calories / 2g fat / 3g protein
15g carbohydrates / 7g fiber

ROASTED MUSHROOMS

MAKES 4 SERVINGS

PREP TIME: 5 MINUTES
COOK TIME: 15 MINUTES

INGREDIENTS

1   tablespoon extra-virgin olive oil

1¼ pounds button mushrooms, sliced

2   cloves garlic, crushed

1   sprig rosemary

    Salt and pepper

1½ teaspoons lemon juice

METHOD

1. Heat the olive oil in a large sauté pan over high heat. When the oil just begins to smoke, add the mushrooms, garlic, and rosemary. Season with salt and pepper. Reduce the heat to medium-high and cook, stirring frequently, until the mushrooms are soft, about 7 minutes.

2. When the mushrooms are cooked and begin to stick to the pan, add the lemon juice and toss one last time. Transfer to a serving dish.

PER SERVING

66 calories / 4g fat / 5g protein
6g carbohydrates / 2g fiber

SPICED CARROTS

MAKES 4 SERVINGS

PREP TIME: 10 MINUTES
COOK TIME: 25 MINUTES

INGREDIENTS

1   tablespoon extra-virgin olive oil
1   pound baby carrots, halved
¼   teaspoon ground cumin
½   teaspoon ground coriander
2   tablespoons lemon juice
½   cup water
¼   cup chopped mint
    Salt and pepper

METHOD

1. Preheat the oven to 400°F.
2. Heat the olive oil in a large sauté pan over high heat. When the oil begins to smoke, add the carrots and cook, stirring frequently, until the carrots begin to brown, about 5 minutes. Sprinkle with the cumin and coriander and stir.
3. Deglaze the pan with the lemon juice. Scrape the carrots into an 8-inch square baking dish, add the water, and cover with foil. Transfer to the oven and cook until tender, about 20 minutes.
4. Remove from the oven. Drain any water that remains. Sprinkle on the mint, season with salt and pepper to taste, and serve.

PER SERVING
74 calories / 4g fat / <1g protein
10g carbohydrates / 2g fiber

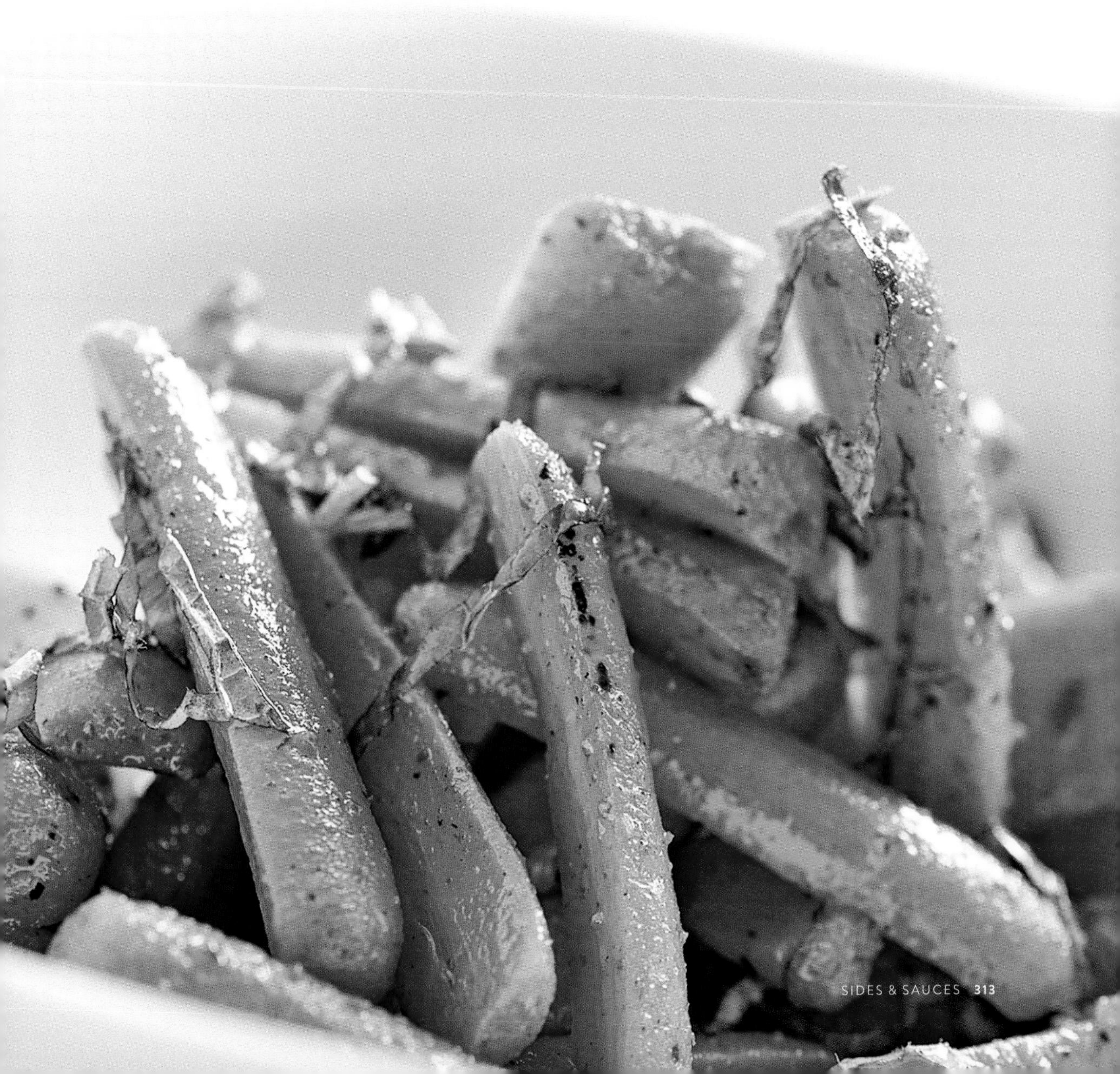

RAW RATATOUILLE

MAKES 4 SERVINGS

Pronounced rah-tah-TOO-ee, the word "ratatouille" stems from *ratatolha*, a name with origins from around Provence and Nice, and *touiller*, the French verb for "toss around." This dish is a vegan's dream, carrying lots of nutrients and a ton of flavor for 54 calories per serving. In my raw version, there's another plus: No cooking required!

PREP TIME: 20 MINUTES
(REFRIGERATE OVERNIGHT)

INGREDIENTS

1   large zucchini, cut into ¼-inch dice
1   medium squash, cut into ¼-inch dice
1   large tomato, diced
½   large red onion, cut into ⅛-inch dice
1   medium yellow bell pepper, cut into
    ¼-inch dice
2   tablespoons lemon juice
1½ tablespoon thyme leaves
½   tablespoon chopped rosemary
    Salt and pepper

METHOD

In a large bowl, combine the zucchini, squash, tomato, onion, bell pepper, lemon juice, thyme, rosemary, and salt and pepper to taste and toss well to combine. Cover and refrigerate overnight for the flavors to blend and the vegetables to soften.

PER SERVING
54 calories / <1g fat / 3g protein
12g carbohydrates / 3g fiber

SNAP PEAS AND MUSHROOMS

MAKES 4 SERVINGS

I just can't help but look at certain vegetables and try to find new and unexpected ways to combine them. So when I started thinking about sweet-tasting snap peas and meaty-flavored mushrooms, I wondered . . . could this be a winning combo? The answer turned out to be a very delicious yes!

PREP TIME: 5 MINUTES
COOK TIME: 10 MINUTES

INGREDIENTS

1   tablespoon extra-virgin olive oil
½   pound cremini mushrooms
¼   pound sugar snap peas
2   cloves garlic, smashed
1½ tablespoons thyme leaves
     Salt and pepper
1   tablespoon white wine vinegar

METHOD

1. Heat the olive oil in a large sauté pan over high heat. When the oil begins to smoke, add the mushrooms, peas, garlic, and thyme. Season with salt and pepper. Cook, tossing frequently, until the mushrooms are softened and browned, about 7 minutes.
2. Deglaze the pan with the vinegar, toss once more, and transfer to a serving dish.

Tip: A note on stringing snap peas: There is a straight and a curved side on a snap pea. Break off the end that would have connected the pea to the plant and pull down the straight edge. A stringy piece will come off the pod.

PER SERVING
60 calories / 4g fat / 3g protein
6g carbohydrates / 1g fiber

CHICKPEA CURRY SAUCE

MAKES 4 SERVINGS

This is a great all-purpose sauce. Use it for dipping raw and cooked veggies and fried foods, or try spreading it on your favorite burger.

PREP TIME: 15 MINUTES

INGREDIENTS

2   cups canned chickpeas
    Juice of 2 lemons
¼   cup water
1   tablespoon extra-virgin olive oil
1   tablespoon curry powder
1   clove garlic

METHOD

In a food processor, combine the chickpeas, lemon juice, water, oil, curry powder, and garlic and process until smooth, about 1 minute.

Tip: You may need more or less curry powder depending on the blend you use.

PER SERVING
87 calories / 4g fat / 3g protein
11g carbohydrates / 2g fiber

SPICY MUSTARD SAUCE

MAKES 1 CUP

For fast flavor, whip up this mustard sauce. It can be paired with fish, sandwiches, burgers, chicken, beef, and more. Its unique flavor comes from the blends of mustards and horseradish.

PREP TIME: 5 MINUTES

INGREDIENTS

¼ cup whole-grain mustard

¼ cup Dijon mustard

½ cup unsweetened nondairy coconut yogurt (such as So Delicious)

2½ teaspoons prepared horseradish

3 packets Monk Fruit in the Raw

METHOD

In a small bowl, mix together the mustards, yogurt, horseradish, and monk fruit.

Tip: Mix in some chopped herbs and serve this sauce over fish (my favorite way to serve it).

PER SERVING
27 calories / 2g fat / <1g protein
2g carbohydrates / 1g fiber

BEST DAMN SAUCE EVER

MAKES ABOUT 1 CUP

A sauce can include almost anything you want it to, and it's fun to experiment. Once I was messing around in my kitchen and ended up with a tantalizing combo of coconut yogurt, unsweetened ketchup, garlic, Worcestershire sauce, pepper, and stevia. It really rocked my world—which is why I named it the Best Damn Sauce Ever. Serve it with Asian-inspired dishes, burgers, baked chicken or pork, even seafood.

PREP TIME: 5 MINUTES

INGREDIENTS

- ½ cup unsweetened nondairy coconut yogurt (such as So Delicious)
- ¼ cup unsweetened ketchup
- 2 cloves garlic, finely grated
- 1 tablespoon Worcestershire sauce
- ¼ teaspoon pepper
- 1 packet Stevia in the Raw

METHOD

In a small bowl, combine the yogurt, ketchup, garlic, Worcestershire sauce, pepper, and stevia. Season with salt and pepper.

PER SERVING
30 calories / <1g fat / 0g protein
6g carbohydrates / <1g fiber

GINGER-SOY DIPPING SAUCE

MAKES 4 SERVINGS

Tired of wasabi and soy for sushi dipping? If you are, have I got a treat for you! The next time sushi is on your menu, whip up this fabulous dipping sauce.

PREP TIME: 10 MINUTES

INGREDIENTS

⅓ cup reduced-sodium tamari

⅓ cup rice vinegar

1 teaspoon sesame oil

1-inch piece fresh ginger, finely grated

3 tablespoons chopped chives

2 packets Monk Fruit in the Raw

METHOD

In a small bowl, thoroughly mix together the tamari, vinegar, sesame oil, ginger, chives, and monk fruit.

Tip: An excellent dipping sauce for sushi and crudos, this stuff is strong, so go easy on it.

PER SERVING
43 calories / 1g fat / 4g protein
3g carbohydrates / <1g fiber

ROCCO'S RAW KETCHUP

MAKES FOUR 4-OUNCE PORTIONS

For me, certain foods aren't nearly as good without ketchup—like meatloaf, hamburgers, and fries. What has always surprised me about ketchup is the amount of sugar in it—even in some organic varieties. Consider: A single tablespoon of ketchup generally yields 20 calories, 16 of which come from sugar. I try to limit sugar, so I invented my own sugar-free ketchup, and it is delicious.

PREP TIME: 10 MINUTES

INGREDIENTS

3   medium tomatoes, cut into chunks
2   tablespoons red wine vinegar
2   packets Stevia in the Raw
1   tablespoon psyllium husk powder

METHOD

In a blender, combine the tomatoes, vinegar, and stevia and puree until smooth, about 1 minute. With the blender running, add the psyllium and continue to blend until the ketchup is thick, about 30 seconds.

Tip: This recipe does not scale well, so I don't recommend doubling or tripling the yield.

PER SERVING
8 calories / <1g fat (0g sat) / <1g protein
2g carbohydrates / 1g fiber

CHAPTER 12

Desserts & Chocolate

FRUIT AND NUT KRISPIE TREAT

MAKES 4 SERVINGS

PREP TIME: 10 MINUTES
SET TIME: 30 MINUTES

INGREDIENTS

½ cup sugar-free marshmallows (such as La Nouba)

2 tablespoons goji berries

2 tablespoons dried mulberries

¼ cup raw pistachios, chopped

¼ cup raw almonds, chopped

METHOD

1. In a microwave-safe bowl, combine the marshmallows, dried fruit, and nuts. Microwave at 70 percent power in 30-second increments, stirring after each, until melted.

2. Transfer the mixture to a sheet of parchment paper and refrigerate for about 30 minutes for the marshmallow to set.

PER SERVING
118 calories / 7g fat / 4g protein
13g carbohydrates / 2g fiber

SUGAR-FREE MARSHMALLOWS

MAKES 12 SQUARES

If you've ever roasted marshmallows (if you haven't, where have you been?), you know that a typical marshmallow is made of sugar, water, and gelation whipped to a spongy consistency and molded into small squarish pieces. Well, here's the same type of recipe, but without the sugar.

PREP TIME: 10 MINUTES
WHIPPING TIME: 15 MINUTES

INGREDIENTS

1½ teaspoons unflavored gelatin

½ cup water

½ cup granular Swerve all-natural sweetener

½ teaspoon vanilla extract

METHOD

1. In a medium bowl, sprinkle the gelatin over ¼ cup of the cold water and set aside for 5 minutes.

2. In a small saucepan, combine the remaining ¼ cup water and the Swerve. Bring to a rolling boil, stirring until the sweetener is dissolved. Remove from the heat and add the vanilla.

3. Slowly whisk the boiling water into the gelatin and stir until all the gelatin is dissolved.

4. Line an 8-inch square pan with parchment paper. In a stand mixer fitted with the whisk attachment, whip the mixture to stiff peaks. Spread the mixture into the lined pan and refrigerate until set.

5. Cut into 1¼-inch squares with a pizza cutter. Eat immediately or refrigerate 20 minutes

Tip: You can chill the marshmallows in the freezer if you wish them to set faster. Just don't forget about them!

PER SERVING
40 calories / 0g fat / <1 protein
10g carbohydrates / 0g fiber

CINNAMON RICE PUDDING

MAKES 4 SERVINGS

Miracle Rice is a low-carb, gluten-free product perfect for rice lovers who cannot eat gluten, soy, or wheat. It absorbs the flavor of whatever it is cooked with. So here, I've used it in a delicious cinnamon pudding, which has a bit of a crunch thanks to the addition of pistachios and goji berries.

PREP TIME: 10 MINUTES
COOK TIME: 15 MINUTES

INGREDIENTS

16 ounces Miracle Rice
½   teaspoon ground cinnamon
¾   cup unsweetened nondairy coconut yogurt (such as So Delicious)
3   packets Monk Fruit in the Raw
¼   cup raw pistachios
2   tablespoons goji berries

METHOD

1. Preheat the oven to 350°F. Line a baking sheet with parchment paper.
2. Rinse the Miracle Rice for 2 minutes under running water. Drain. Place on the lined baking sheet and bake for 15 minutes in order to dry it out. Remove from the oven.
3. In a medium bowl, combine the Miracle Rice, cinnamon, yogurt, monk fruit, pistachios, and goji berries. Mix well and serve.

PER SERVING
77 calories / 4.5g fat / 2g protein
7g carbohydrates / 2g fiber

BLUEBERRY-ALMOND PARFAIT

MAKES 4 SERVINGS (½ CUP EACH)

PREP TIME: 15 MINUTES
COOK TIME: 5 MINUTES

INGREDIENTS

2   cups blueberries

1   brown rice cake

½   cup unsweetened nondairy coconut yogurt (such as So Delicious)

4   packets Monk Fruit in the Raw

¼   cup raw almonds, chopped

METHOD

1. Place the blueberries in a small saucepan and cook over high heat just until they begin to burst and release their juices, about 5 minutes. Transfer to a bowl and place in the freezer to cool quickly.

2. Crush the brown rice cake with your fingers and place it in a small bowl. Stir in ¼ cup of the yogurt and 2 packets of the monk fruit.

3. In another small bowl, mix the remaining ¼ cup yogurt and 2 packets monk fruit.

4. To build the parfaits, divide the rice cake mixture evenly in the bottoms of 4 small glasses. Spoon the blueberries on top of this. Top the blueberries with the yogurt, and finish it off with the chopped almonds.

PER SERVING
113 calories / 5g fat / 3g protein
17g carbohydrates / 3g fiber

KEY LIME MOUSSE WITH CHOCOLATE SAUCE

MAKES 4 SERVINGS

If you love mousse-type desserts but have never used avocados to create the creamy consistency of mousse, here's your chance. Avocado is not just for salads and sandwiches anymore! Note that if you can't find key limes, you can substitute regular limes in this recipe and it will still be just as delicious!

PREP TIME: 15 MINUTES

INGREDIENTS

2   avocados

2   teaspoons grated key lime zest

2   tablespoons key lime juice

9   packets Monk Fruit in the Raw

1   cup water

3   tablespoons unsweetened raw cacao powder

¼   teaspoon xanthan gum

¼   cup chopped mint

METHOD

1. In a blender, combine the avocados, lime zest, lime juice, and 3 packets of the monk fruit and puree until smooth, about 60 seconds. Transfer to a bowl and clean the blender.

2. In the blender, combine the remaining 6 packets monk fruit, the water, cacao powder, and xanthan gum and puree until the mixture thickens, about 30 seconds.

3. Portion the lime mousse into serving bowls and top with some of the chocolate sauce and mint.

PER SERVING
112 calories / 10g fat / 1g protein
8g carbohydrates / 6g fiber

BANANA SPLIT POPS

MAKES 4 POPS

Once upon a time, I went to a big culinary school and worked in fancy restaurants. Now, I'm cooking for myself, my readers, and my clients—and creating healthy and delicious dishes for them, like these simple, delicious ice pops.

PREP TIME: 5 MINUTES
FREEZE TIME: 3 HOURS

INGREDIENTS

2   green bananas, broken into pieces
½   cup unsweetened coconut milk beverage (such as So Delicious)
2   packets Monk Fruit in the Raw
¼   teaspoon xanthan gum
¼   cup finely diced strawberries
2   tablespoons cacao nibs

METHOD

1. In a blender, combine the bananas, coconut milk, and monk fruit and puree on high until smooth, about 45 seconds.
2. With the blender running, add the xanthan gum and puree until the mixture thickens, another 15 to 30 seconds.
3. Transfer to a bowl and fold in the strawberries and cacao nibs. Pour into ice pop molds and freeze for at least 3 hours.

PER POP

91 calories / 2g fat / <1g protein
20g carbohydrates / 3g fiber

CHERRY-ALMOND ICE POPS

MAKES 4 POPS

Artificial cherry flavoring is everywhere in the candy aisle, but it pales in comparison to the real thing. You can get so much more flavor and goodness (and nutrients) from fresh cherries. In this recipe, your hankering for cherry flavor will definitely be satisfied.

PREP TIME: 5 MINUTES
FREEZE TIME: 3 HOURS

INGREDIENTS

¾   pound fresh cherries
¼   cup unsweetened almond milk (such as Califia Farms)
¼   cup unsweetened nondairy coconut yogurt (such as So Delicious)
6   packets Monk Fruit in the Raw
    Pinch of salt
¼   teaspoon xanthan gum

METHOD

1. In a blender, combine the cherries, almond milk, yogurt, monk fruit, and salt and puree on high until smooth, about 30 seconds.
2. With the blender running, add the xanthan gum and puree until the mixture tightens up, about 30 seconds.
3. Pour into ice pop molds and freeze for at least 3 hours.

PER POP

65 calories / <1g fat / <1g protein
15g carbohydrates / 2g fiber

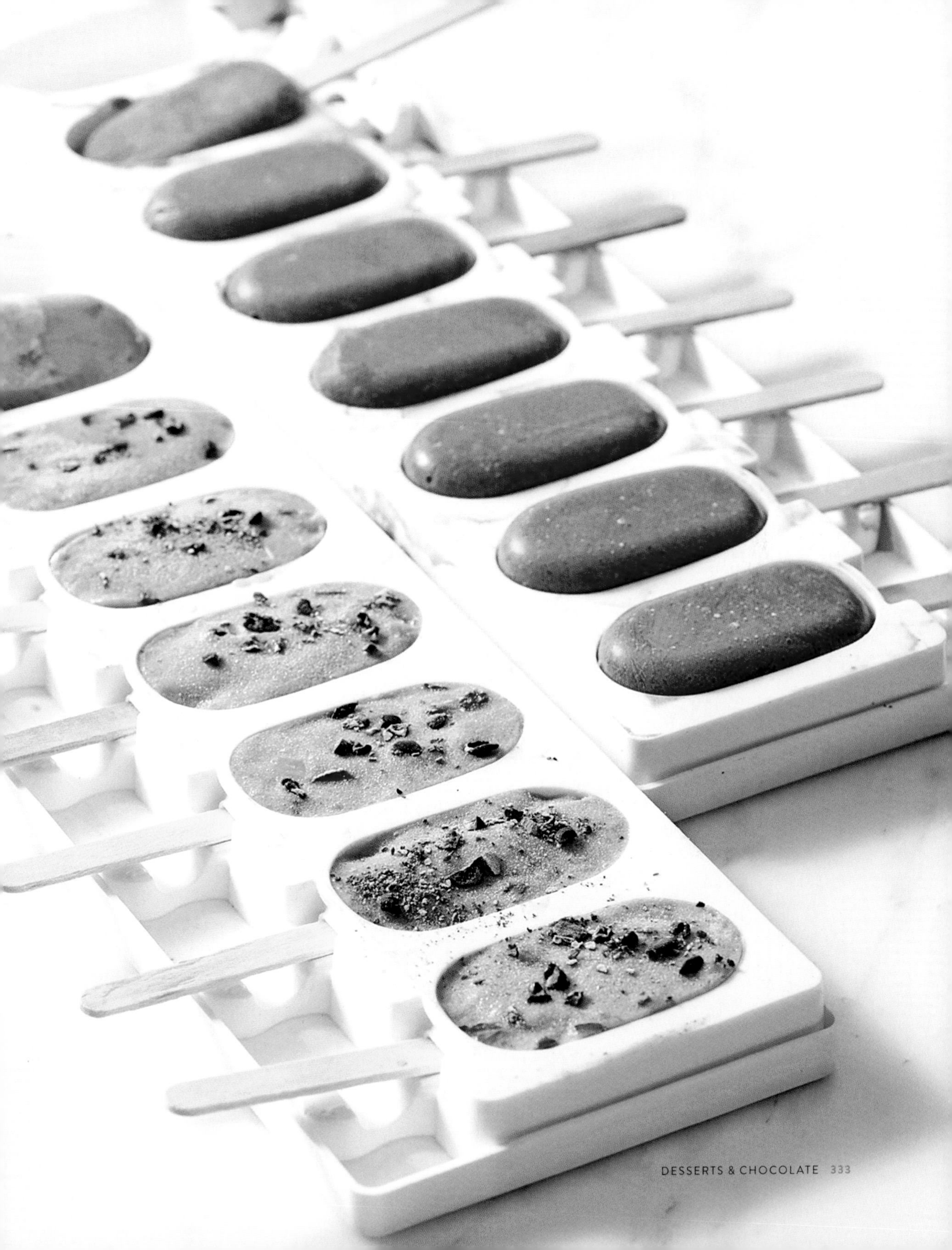

HAZELNUT, GOJI, AND COCONUT COOKIES

MAKES 4 LARGE OR 8 SMALL COOKIES

I created these cookies with goji berries because they are full of antioxidants and are considered a superfruit. The addition of hazelnut flour lends a very sweet, nutty taste; the coconut, a tropical touch.

PREP TIME: 10 MINUTES
COOK TIME: 12 MINUTES

INGREDIENTS

¼ cup hazelnut meal/flour
2 tablespoons goji berries
¼ cup unsweetened coconut flakes
2 packets Monk Fruit in the Raw
3 tablespoons egg white

METHOD

1. Preheat the oven to 350°F. Line a baking sheet with parchment paper.
2. In a medium bowl, combine the hazelnut meal, goji berries, coconut flakes, monk fruit, and egg white and mix well to combine.
3. Portion onto a lined baking sheet with a tablespoon measure. Bake until the centers of the cookies are set, about 12 minutes. Let cool on the baking sheet or eat warm.

PER SERVING
94 calories / 5g fat / 3g protein
8g carbohydrates / 2g fiber

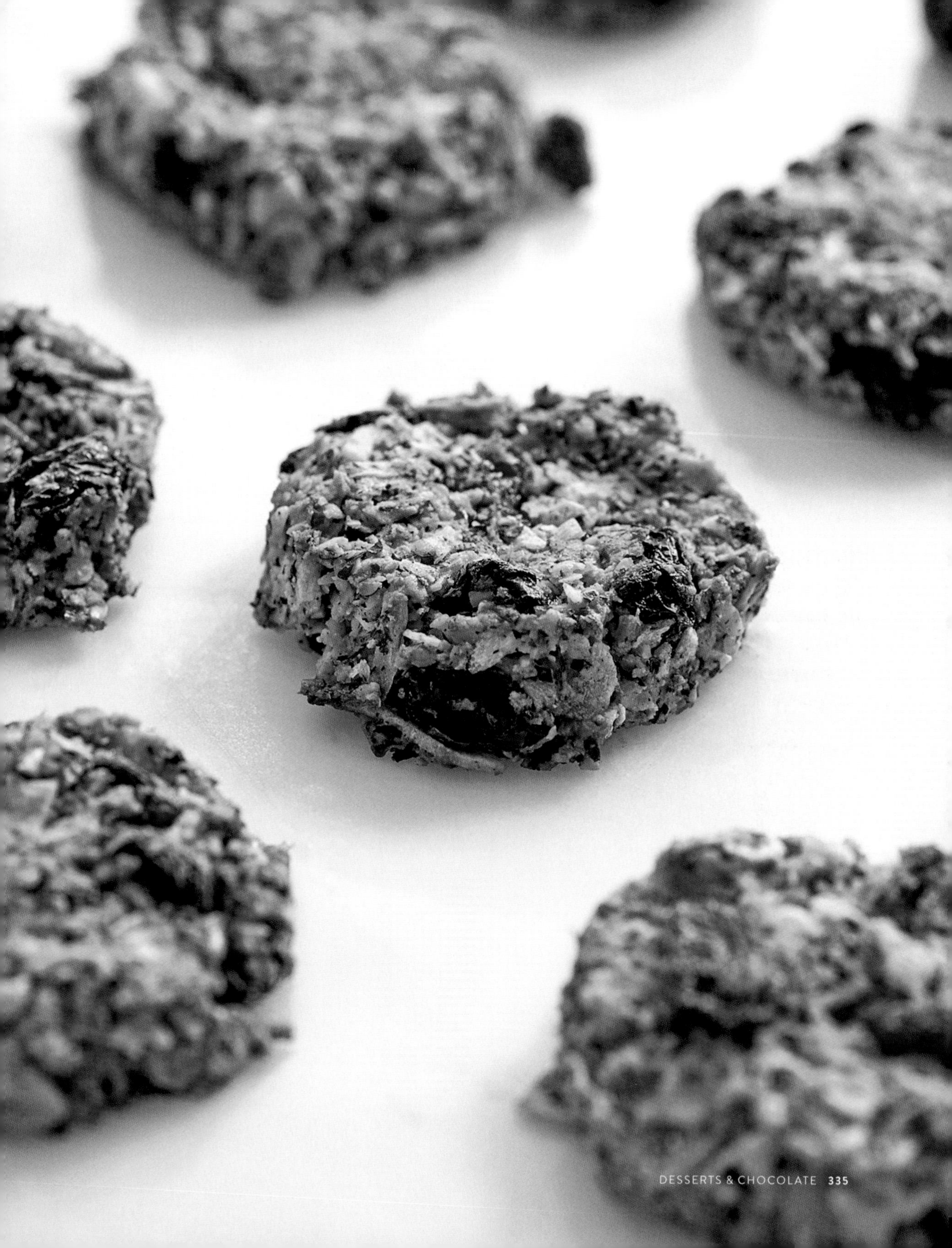

CHOCOLATE-BLUEBERRY COOKIES

MAKES 12 COOKIES (3 PER SERVING)

───────────────

PREP TIME: 10 MINUTES
COOK TIME: 12 MINUTES

INGREDIENTS

1   cup canned black beans, drained and rinsed

2   tablespoons raw coconut nectar

⅓   cup unsweetened cocoa powder

8   packets Monk Fruit in the Raw

¾   cup liquid egg whites

½   cup blueberries

⅓   cup stevia-sweetened chocolate chips (such as Lily's)

METHOD

1. Preheat the oven to 375°F. Line a baking sheet with parchment paper.

2. In a food processor, combine the black beans, coconut nectar, cocoa powder, and monk fruit. Pulse until smooth and the mixture forms a ball in the bowl of the machine.

3. In a bowl, with an electric mixer, whip the egg whites to stiff peaks.

4. Place one-third of the egg whites in the food processor and mix into the chocolate mixture. Transfer the dough to a large bowl and fold in the rest of the egg whites in two additions.

5. Fold the blueberries into the dough. Drop by the spoonful onto the lined baking sheet to form twelve 2-inch-diameter cookies. Place 5 chocolate chips onto each cookie.

6. Bake until firm around the edges, about 12 minutes. Let cool on sheet.

PER SERVING
129 calories / 2g fat / 8g protein
25g carbohydrates / 7g fiber

NO-BAKE CHOCOLATE CHIP COOKIES

MAKES 4 SERVINGS

Cookie dough served up in a dish is all the rage where I live. Well, this recipe is just as good. You mold the batter into cookies, but it's okay if you take a few swipes with your spoon, too.

PREP TIME: 10 MINUTES

INGREDIENTS

¼ cup unsweetened shredded coconut

¼ cup almond meal/flour

2 tablespoons unsweetened almond butter

½ teaspoon vanilla extract

2 tablespoons stevia-sweetened chocolate chips (such as Lily's)

1 tablespoon raw coconut nectar

METHOD

In a medium bowl, combine the shredded coconut, almond meal, almond butter, vanilla, chocolate chips, and coconut nectar and mix well with your hands. Form into 8 balls, then press into round disks with the palm of your hand.

PER SERVING
153 calories / 11g fat / 4g protein
12g carbohydrates / 4g fiber

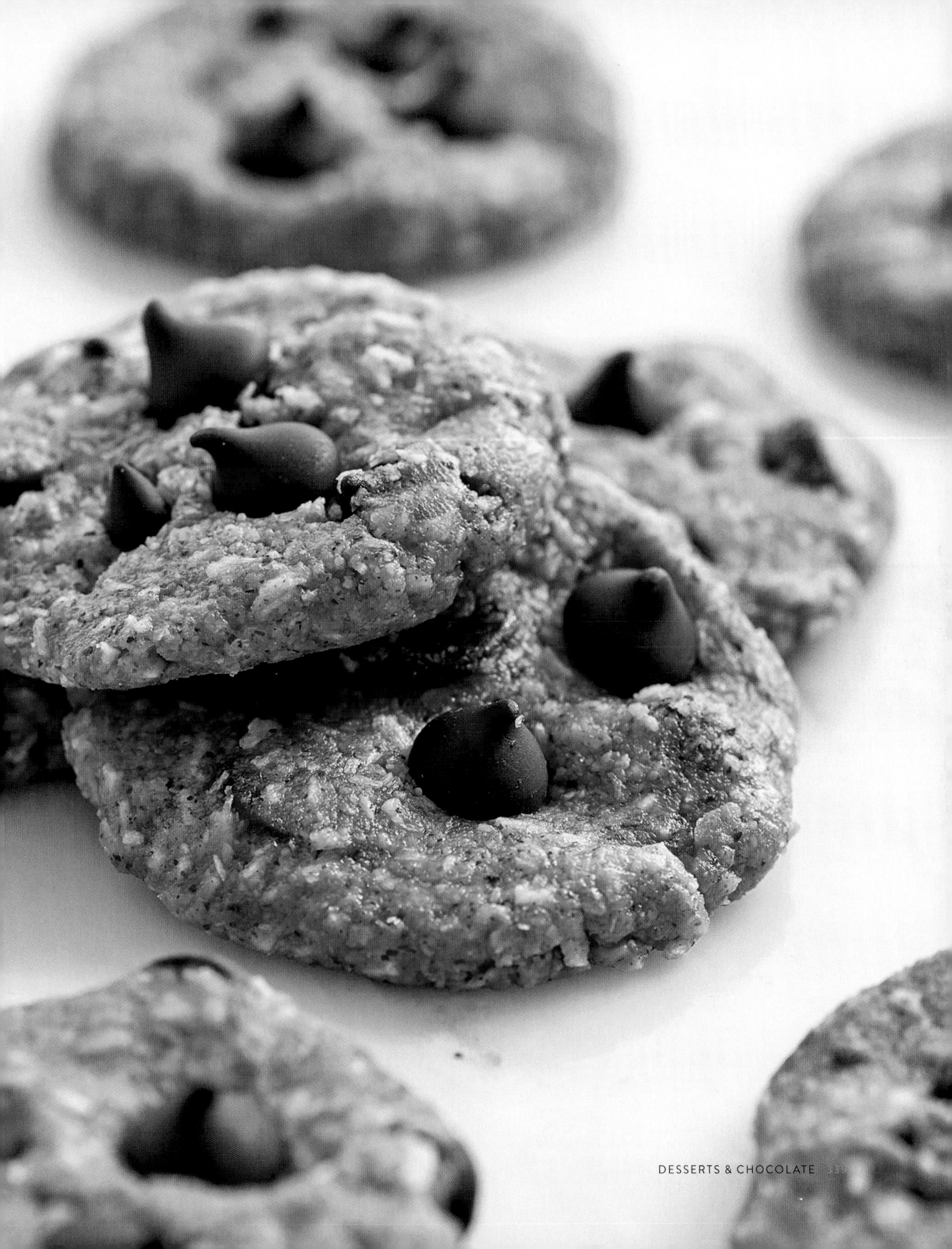

CHOCOLATE CHIP OATMEAL COOKIES

MAKES 4 SERVINGS

_____

PREP TIME: 10 MINUTES

INGREDIENTS

¼ cup rolled oats

2 tablespoons stevia-sweetened chocolate chips (such as Lily's)

2 packets Monk Fruit in the Raw

2 tablespoons coconut flour

2 tablespoons unsweetened almond butter

2 teaspoons coconut oil, melted

METHOD

1. In a medium bowl, combine the oats, chocolate chips, monk fruit, and coconut flour and toss to combine.

2. Add the almond butter and coconut oil and mix well. Form into 12 balls, press into a cookie shape with your palm, and refrigerate.

Tip: If the mixture becomes too warm to work with, place it in the refrigerator for a few minutes, then resume shaping the cookies.

PER SERVING
133 calories / 9g fat / 4g protein
11g carbohydrates / 5g fiber

ALMOND BUTTER–OATMEAL CHOCOLATE COOKIES

MAKES 4 SERVINGS

_____

PREP TIME: 10 MINUTES

INGREDIENTS

2 tablespoons unsweetened almond butter

½ cup rolled oats

2 teaspoons unsweetened cocoa powder

1 tablespoon raw coconut nectar

2 packets Monk Fruit in the Raw

METHOD

1. In a medium bowl, combine the almond butter, oats, cocoa powder, coconut nectar, and monk fruit and combine well.

2. Form into 8 balls, and press down on them with the palm of your hand to achieve a cookie shape.

Tip: Refrigerate the mixture for a few minutes if the heat from your hands makes it difficult to work with.

PER SERVING
107 calories / 5g fat / 3g protein
12g carbohydrates / 2g fiber

OATMEAL-WALNUT COOKIES

MAKES 4 SERVINGS

PREP TIME: 10 MINUTES

INGREDIENTS

¼ cup almond meal/flour

¼ cup rolled oats

2 tablespoons chopped walnuts

4 packets Monk Fruit in the Raw

½ teaspoon ground cinnamon

2 tablespoons unsweetened almond butter

1½ teaspoons coconut oil, melted

METHOD

1. In a medium bowl, combine the almond meal, rolled oats, walnuts, monk fruit, and cinnamon and toss to combine.

2. Add the almond butter and coconut oil and mix well. Place in the refrigerator for a few minutes to allow the mixture to firm up.

3. Mold into 8 cookies. Store in the refrigerator.

PER SERVING

152 calories / 11g fat / 5g protein

7g carbohydrates / 2g fiber

SUN-BUTTER CHOCOLATE CHIP COOKIES

MAKES 4 SERVINGS

PREP TIME: 10 MINUTES
COOK TIME: 13 MINUTES

INGREDIENTS

⅔ cup canned chickpeas, drained and rinsed

4 tablespoons unsweetened sunflower seed butter (such as Once Again)

6 packets Monk Fruit in the Raw

4 teaspoons water

1 teaspoon vanilla extract

1 teaspoon baking powder

¼ cup stevia-sweetened chocolate chips (such as Lily's)

METHOD

1. Preheat the oven to 350°F. Line a baking sheet with parchment paper.
2. In a food processor, combine the chickpeas, sunflower seed butter, monk fruit, water, vanilla, and baking powder. Pulse 4 times to get the mixture moving, then let it run until smooth, about 1 minute.
3. Transfer the dough to a medium bowl and mix in the chocolate chips with a rubber spatula. Scoop into 1-inch mounds on the lined baking sheet.
4. Bake until set, about 13 minutes. Let cool.

PER SERVING
176 calories / 3g fat / 6g protein
14g carbohydrates / 5g fiber

HAZELNUT SPREAD COOKIES

MAKES 4 SERVINGS

When hazelnut and coconut marry, it's a match made in cookie heaven. So creamy, so delicious, these no-bake cookies won't last long in your house!

PREP TIME: 10 MINUTES

INGREDIENTS

- ¼ cup hazelnut meal/flour
- ¼ cup unsweetened shredded coconut
- 2 tablespoons low-sugar chocolate hazelnut spread (such as Rocco's)
- 1 tablespoon raw coconut nectar

PER SERVING
103 calories / 8g fat / 2g protein
7g carbohydrates / 1g fiber

METHOD

1. In a medium bowl, combine the hazelnut meal and coconut. Add the hazelnut spread and coconut nectar and mix well.
2. Form into 8 cookie-shaped balls and refrigerate.

Tips: If the spread is too firm to mix in, place it in the microwave for 1 minute, stirring at 30 seconds.

ALMOND-COCONUT COOKIES

MAKES 4 SERVINGS

PREP TIME: 10 MINUTES

INGREDIENTS

1   scoop protein powder
    (such as Rocco's Protein Powder Plus)
¼   cup raw almonds, chopped
1   teaspoon unsweetened cocoa
    powder
¼   cup unsweetened
    shredded coconut
¼   cup almond meal/flour
¼   cup water

METHOD

In a medium bowl, toss together the protein powder, almonds, cocoa powder, coconut, and almond meal. Add the water and mix well. Form into 8 balls and refrigerate.

PER SERVING
130 calories / 9g fat / 9g protein
6g carbohydrates / 4g fiber

SNICKERDOODLE PROTEIN BALLS

MAKES 4 SERVINGS

PREP TIME: 10 MINUTES

INGREDIENTS

¼ cup coconut flour

1 scoop protein powder (such as Rocco's Protein Powder Plus)

1 teaspoon ground cinnamon

½ cup water

1 tablespoon Swerve confectioners sweetener

METHOD

1. In a small bowl, toss together the coconut flour, protein powder, and ½ teaspoon of the cinnamon. Pour in the water and mix well. Form into 8 balls.

2. In a second bowl, mix the remaining ½ teaspoon cinnamon with the Swerve sweetener and roll each ball in it to coat.

PER SERVING
57 calories / <1g fat / 6g protein
10g carbohydrates / 5g fiber

COCONUT MACAROONS

MAKES 4 SERVINGS

As a coconut lover, I've experimented with lots of coconut macaroon recipes over the years. This recipe is my favorite, especially with the addition of cacao nibs. Like typical macaroons, these are chewy and moist. They also keep well, which makes them great for snacks.

PREP TIME: 10 MINUTES

INGREDIENTS

1   cup unsweetened shredded coconut
2   teaspoons raw coconut nectar
¼   teaspoon vanilla extract
1   tablespoon cacao nibs

METHOD

1. In a blender, combine the shredded coconut, coconut nectar, and vanilla and pulse until the coconut begins to break down and form a solid mass, about 8 times.
2. Transfer to a bowl and stir in the cacao nibs.
3. Drop by the tablespoon onto a piece of parchment and form into haystack shapes with your fingers.

PER MACAROON
85 calories / 6g fat / 1g protein
6g carbohydrates / 2g fiber

CHOCOLATE-ALMOND-COCONUT BALLS

MAKES 4 SERVINGS

This no-bake dessert is the result of one of my many experiments with almond meal and various forms of coconut. In this case, the addition of chocolate makes them slightly reminiscent of a certain "joyful" candy bar.

PREP TIME: 10 MINUTES

INGREDIENTS

- ¼ cup almond meal/flour
- ¼ cup unsweetened shredded coconut
- 1 tablespoon coconut oil, melted
- 2 tablespoons stevia-sweetened chocolate chips (such as Lily's)
- ½ teaspoon vanilla extract
- 1 teaspoon raw coconut nectar

METHOD

In a large bowl, combine the almond meal, shredded coconut, coconut oil, chocolate chips, vanilla, and coconut nectar. Mix well with your hands, and form into 8 balls. Refrigerate.

PER SERVING

118 calories / 10g fat / 2g protein
8g carbohydrates / 3g fiber

CHOCOLATE PROTEIN TRUFFLES

MAKES 4 SERVINGS

———————————

PREP TIME: 10 MINUTES

INGREDIENTS

1   avocado

1   scoop protein powder
(such as Rocco's Protein Powder Plus)

1   tablespoon unsweetened cocoa powder

½   teaspoon vanilla extract

4   packets Monk Fruit in the Raw

METHOD

1. In a food processor, combine the avocado, protein powder, cocoa, vanilla, and monk fruit and pulse to combine.
2. Roll into 12 balls.

PER SERVING
85 calories / 5g fat / 6g protein
5g carbohydrates / 5g fiber

PROTEIN CAKE BITES

MAKES 4 SERVINGS

———————————

PREP TIME: 10 MINUTES

INGREDIENTS

1 scoop protein powder
   (such as Rocco's Protein Powder Plus)
¼ cup coconut flour
2 tablespoons coconut oil, melted
1 teaspoon vanilla extract
3 packets Monk Fruit in the Raw
¼ cup water

METHOD

1. In a small bowl, combine the protein powder, coconut flour, coconut oil, vanilla, monk fruit, and water and mix with fork until combined.
2. Roll into 8 balls and refrigerate.

Tip: These are great rolled in dried fruit or nuts.

PER SERVING
117 calories / 7g fat / 6g protein
6g carbohydrates / 4g fiber

FRUIT WITH STEVIA

MAKES 4 SERVINGS

PREP TIME: 5 MINUTES

INGREDIENTS

4   small plums, pitted and cut into bite-size
    pieces
2   tablespoons chopped fresh stevia or
    1 packet Stevia in the Raw

METHOD

Divide the plums among 4 bowls and
sprinkle with the stevia.

PER SERVING
63 calories / <1g fat / 1g protein
15g carbohydrates / 2g fiber

EARL GREY HEMP HEART BARK

MAKES 4 SERVINGS

Hemp may be best known for its narcotic element, but don't worry—this recipe is not my rendition of marijuana brownies. Hemp hearts are a fantastic source of plant-based protein, making this chocolate bark a great stand-in as a healthy snack, too!

PREP TIME: 10 MINUTES
SET TIME: 10 MINUTES

INGREDIENTS

1½ teaspoons Earl Grey tea leaves
½   cup stevia-sweetened chocolate chips (such as Lily's)
1   teaspoon coconut oil
1   teaspoon hemp hearts

METHOD

1. Steep the tea leaves according to the package directions. Drain the leaves (and discard or drink the liquid) and place the leaves between a few layers of paper towels to get the moisture out of them.

2. In a microwave-safe bowl, combine the chocolate chips and coconut oil and microwave for 30 seconds, then stir. Microwave another 30 seconds and stir again. If the chocolate is not melted at this point, begin microwaving it in 15-second increments, stirring after each one until the chocolate is melted.

3. Line a baking sheet with parchment paper. Pour the chocolate onto the lined baking sheet and spread it around with a spatula until you get a thin layer. Sprinkle the tea leaves and hemp hearts on top. Transfer to the freezer for 10 minutes to harden.

4. To serve, break into large pieces with your hands.

PER SERVING
114 calories / 10g fat / 2g protein
18g carbohydrates / 8g fiber

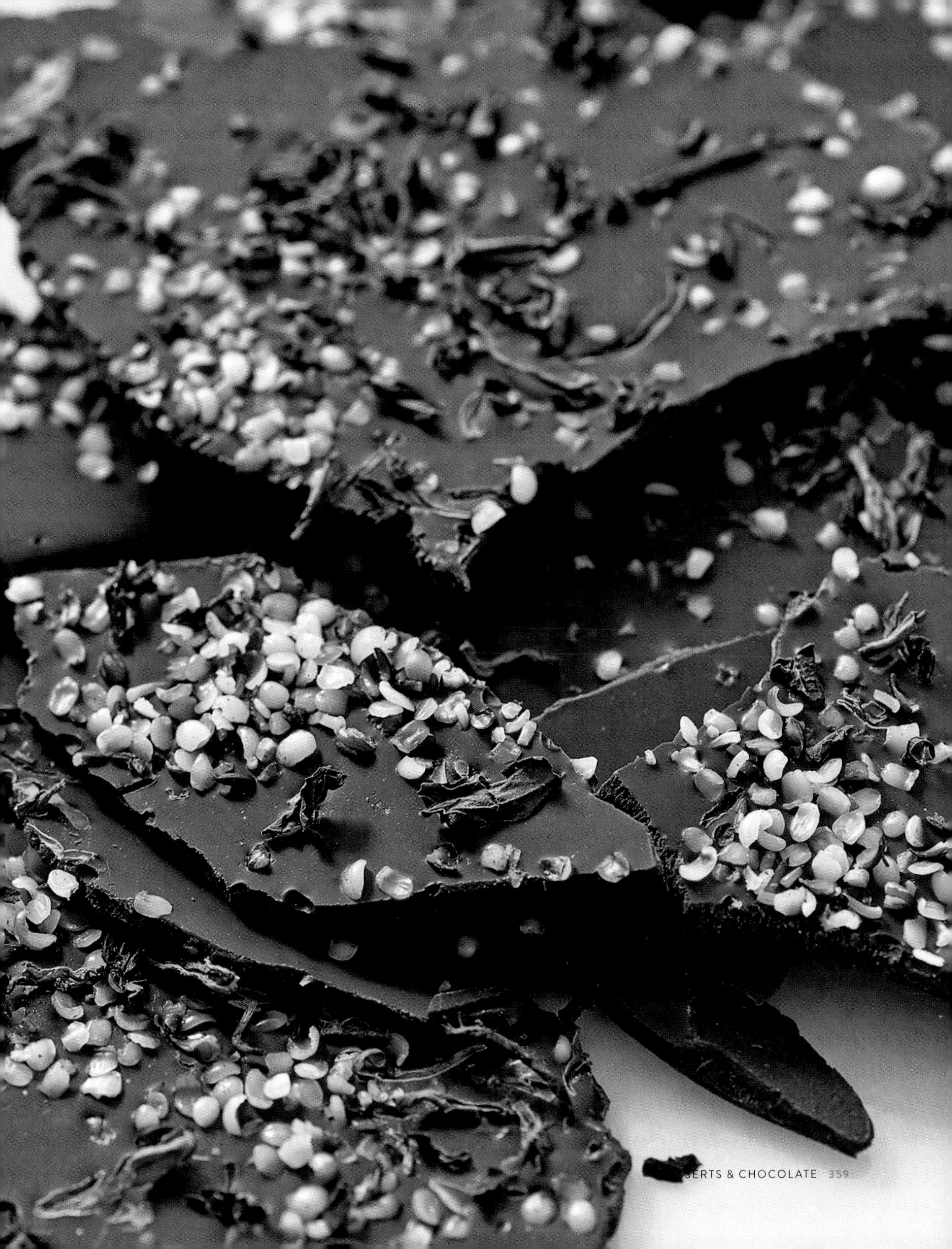

COCONUT-ESPRESSO BARK

MAKES 4 SERVINGS

___

I love making barks; there's nothing to it. You simply melt chocolate, spread it out, and add your favorite ingredients. One of mine is espresso powder; it amplifies the chocolate-ness and gives you a little pick-me-up.

PREP TIME: 5 MINUTES
SET TIME: 10 MINUTES

INGREDIENTS

½ cup stevia-sweetened chocolate chips (such as Lily's)

1 teaspoon coconut oil

1 teaspoon instant espresso powder (such as Medagalia d'Oro)

2 tablespoons unsweetened coconut chips

METHOD

1. In a microwave-safe bowl, combine the chocolate chips and coconut oil and microwave for 30 seconds, then stir. Microwave another 30 seconds and stir again. If the chocolate is not melted at this point, begin microwaving it in 15-second increments, stirring after each one until the chocolate is melted.

2. Line a baking sheet with parchment paper. Pour the chocolate onto the lined baking sheet and spread it around with a spatula until you get a thin layer. Sprinkle the espresso powder and coconut chips on top and transfer to the freezer to harden, about 10 minutes. Break the bark into pieces and store in the refrigerator.

PER SERVING
122 calories / 11g fat / 2g protein
18g carbohydrates / 8g fiber

SPICY PISTACHIO-GOJI BARK

MAKES 4 SERVINGS

———————

PREP TIME: 10 MINUTES
SET TIME: 10 MINUTES

INGREDIENTS

4 ounces stevia-sweetened chocolate chips (such as Lily's)
1 teaspoon coconut oil
Cayenne pepper
¼ cup raw pistachios, chopped
2 tablespoons goji berries

METHOD

1. In a microwave-safe bowl, combine the chocolate and coconut oil and microwave for 30 seconds, then stir. Microwave another 30 seconds and stir again. If the chocolate is not melted at this point, begin microwaving it in 15-second increments, stirring after each one until the chocolate is melted. Stir in as much cayenne pepper as you would like.

2. Line a baking sheet with parchment paper. Pour the melted chocolate onto the lined baking sheet and spread the chocolate into a thin, even layer with a spatula. Sprinkle the pistachios and goji berries on top of the chocolate and tap the tray a few times to get the toppings to adhere. Transfer to the freezer for about 10 minutes to harden.

3. To serve, break into large pieces with your hands.

PER SERVING
165 calories / 13g fat / 4g protein
23g carbohydrates / 9g fiber

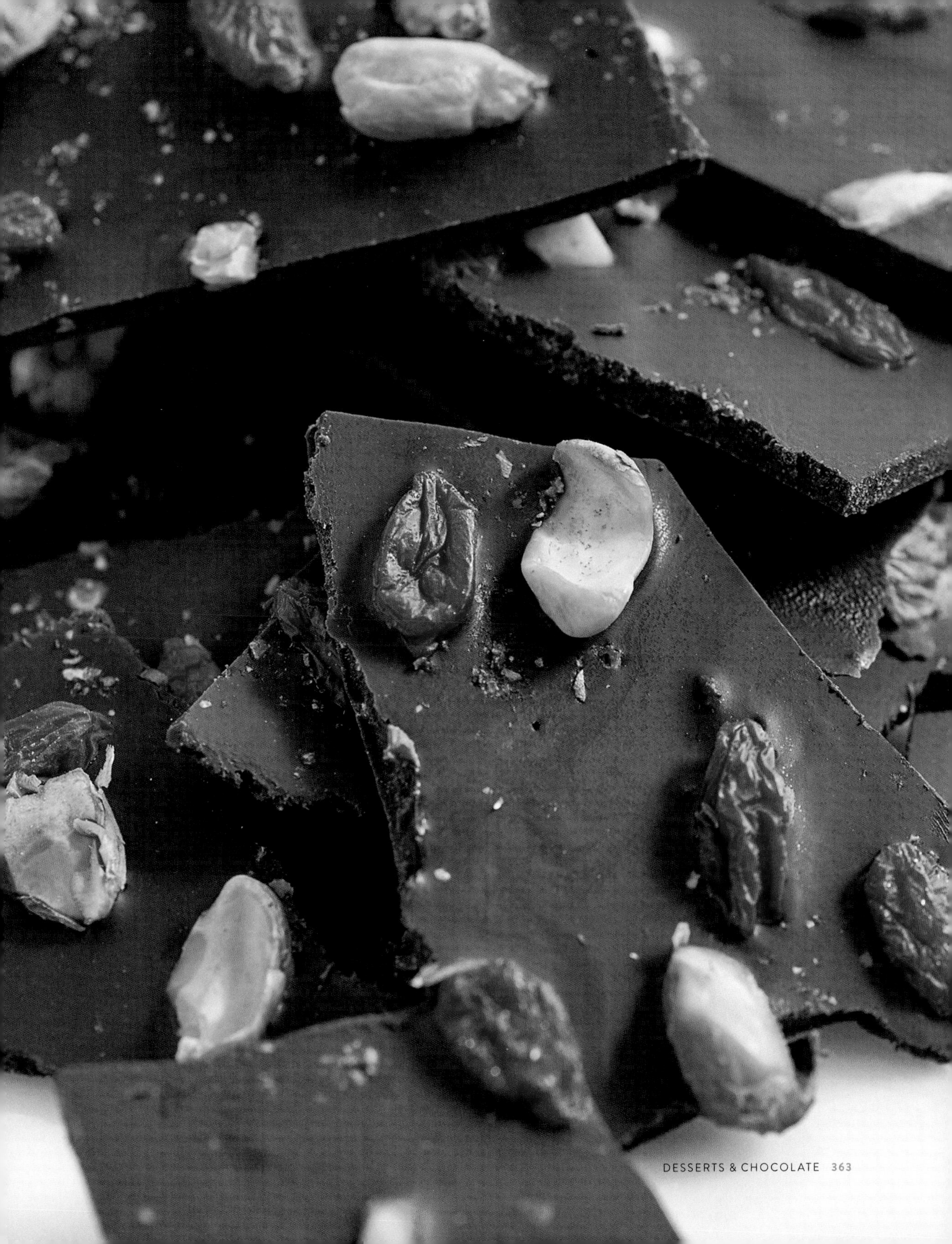

MULBERRY-WALNUT BARK

MAKES 4 SERVINGS

PREP TIME: 5 MINUTES
SET TIME: 10 MINUTES

INGREDIENTS

4   ounces stevia-sweetened chocolate chips
    (such as Lily's)
1   teaspoon coconut oil
¼   cup chopped raw walnuts
2   tablespoons dried mulberries

METHOD

1. In a microwave-safe bowl, combine the chocolate and coconut oil and microwave for 30 seconds, then stir. Microwave another 30 seconds and stir again. If the chocolate is not melted at this point, begin microwaving it in 15-second increments, stirring after each one until the chocolate is melted.

2. Line a baking sheet with parchment paper. Pour the melted chocolate onto the lined baking sheet and spread the chocolate into a thin, even layer with a spatula. Sprinkle the walnuts and mulberries on top of the chocolate and tap the tray a few times to get the toppings to adhere. Transfer to the freezer for 10 minutes to harden.

3. To serve, break into large pieces with your hands.

PER SERVING
166 calories / 14g fat / 3g protein
22g carbohydrates / 9g fiber

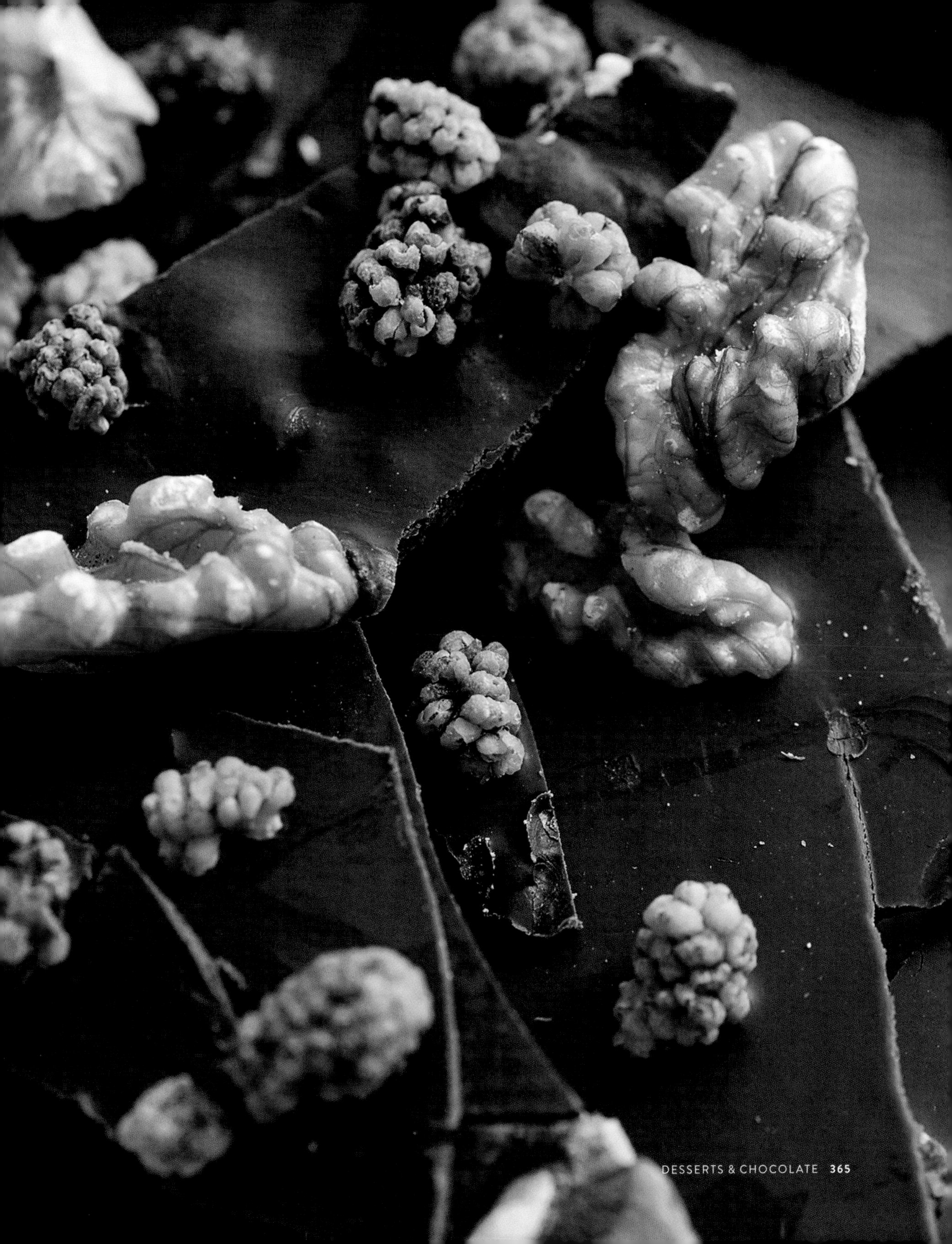

COCONUT-ALMOND BARK

MAKES 4 SERVINGS

———————————

PREP TIME: 5 MINUTES
SET TIME: 15 MINUTES

INGREDIENTS

4   ounces stevia-sweetened chocolate
    (such as Lily's), roughly chopped

1   tablespoon coconut oil

1   packet Stevia in the Raw

2   tablespoons chopped raw almonds

2   tablespoons unsweetened coconut flakes

METHOD

1. In a microwave-safe bowl, combine the chocolate and coconut oil and microwave for 30 seconds, then stir. Microwave another 30 seconds and stir again. If the chocolate is not melted at this point, begin microwaving it in 15-second increments, stirring after each one until the chocolate is melted. Mix in the stevia.

2. Line a baking sheet with parchment paper. Pour the melted chocolate onto the lined baking sheet and spread the chocolate into an ½-inch thick, even layer with a spatula. Sprinkle the almonds and coconut flakes on top of the chocolate and tap the tray a few times to get the toppings to adhere. Refrigerate for about 15 minutes to harden.

3. To serve, break into large pieces with your hands.

PER SERVING
174 calories / 16g fat / 3g protein
20g carbohydrates / 9g fiber

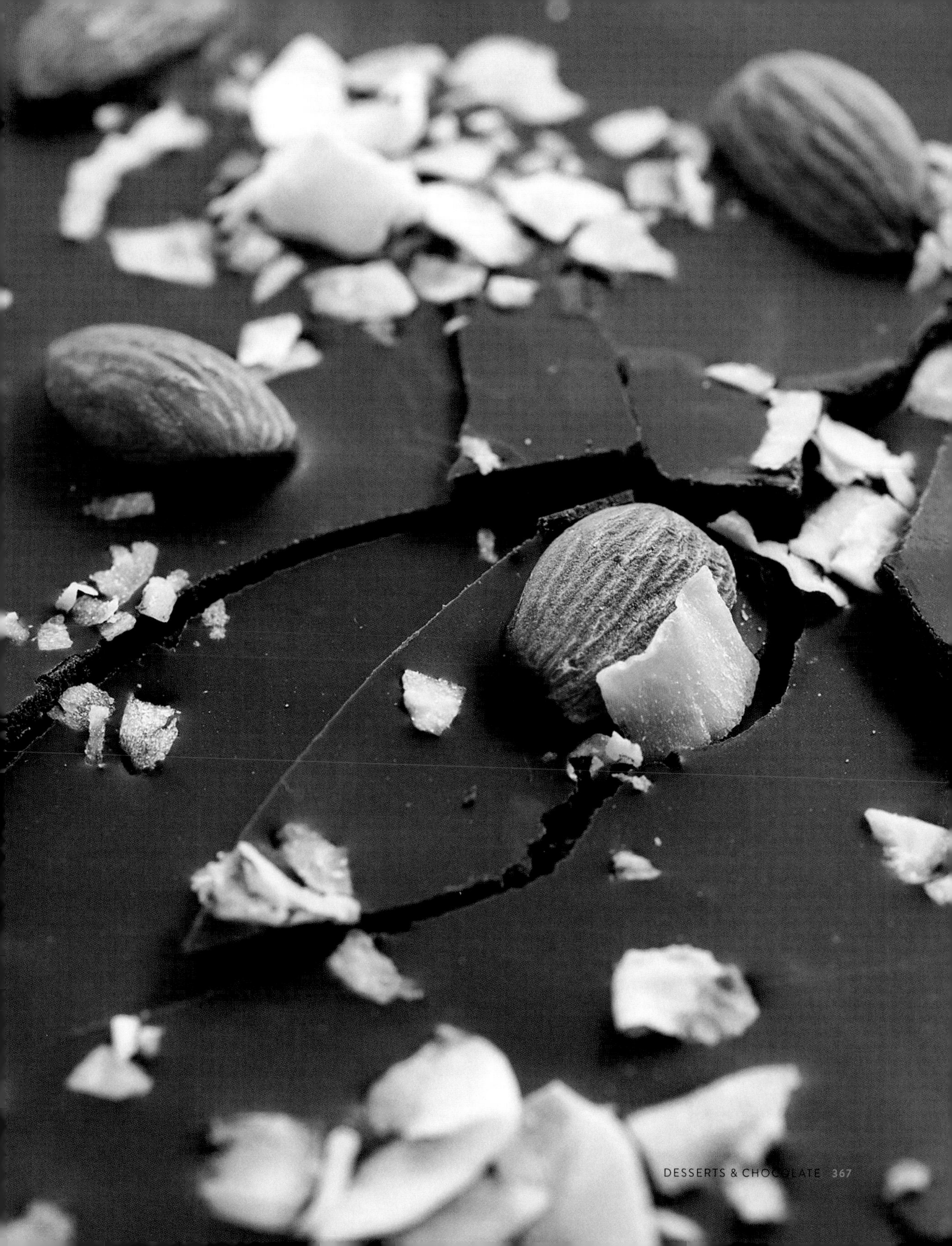

ALMOND BRITTLE

MAKES 4 SERVINGS

PREP TIME: 5 MINUTES
COOK TIME: 5 MINUTES
SET TIME: 30 MINUTES

INGREDIENTS

1½ tablespoons raw coconut nectar

6   packets Stevia in the Raw
     Pinch of salt

1   teaspoon vanilla extract

½   cup raw almonds

METHOD

1. Line a small baking sheet with a piece of parchment.

2. In small pot, combine the coconut nectar, stevia, and salt. Stir over high heat until it comes to a boil. Simmer for 5 minutes, or until reduced by half and remove from the heat. Stir in the vanilla and almonds.

3. Spread on the lined baking sheet and set out to harden for 30 minutes. Break into pieces and serve.

PER SERVING
109 calories / 8g fat / 4g protein
8g carbohydrates / 2g fiber

INDEX

Page numbers of illustrations appear in italics.

celery
  Beef and Red Lentil Soup, 112, *113*
  Cajun Veggie Burgers, *161*, 166
  Coconut-Cilantro Chicken Soup, 118, *119*
  Herb Lentil Salad, 148, *149*
  Roasted Cornish Game Hen, 204, *204*
  Shrimp Creole, 188, *189*
  Shrimp Salad with Juniper and Cucumber,
    150, *151*
  Stuffed Zucchini, 206, *207*
  Celery Root Salad, Avocado and, 287, *287*
cereals. *See also* oats, rolled
  Cinnamon Mulberry Crisp, 58, *59*
  Protein Cereal Bars, 72–73, *72*
ceviche, 244, 246
  Asian-Style Ceviche, 246, *247*
  Ceviche with Leche de Tigre, 248, *248*
  Shrimp and Scallop Ceviche, 244, *245*
chard
  Raw Chard Tacos, 236, *237*
  Roasted Beet Salad, 128, *129*
cheese, nondairy, 8
  Bacon, Egg, and Cheese Breakfast Sandwich,
    48, *49*
  Smoked Salmon with Herbed Cashew Cheese,
    54, 55
cherries and dried cherries
  Black Forest Trail Mix, 276, *276*
  Cherry-Almond Ice Pops, 332, *333*
chia seeds, 11
  Beet, Red Pepper, and Apple Juice, 98, *98*
  Berry Lemonade Chia Drink, 98, *98*
  Cranapple Chia Drink, 94, *94*
  Fruity Almond and Chia Sandwich, 52, *53*
  Peach and Ginger Chia Drink, 95, *95*
  Pomegranate Chia Overnight Oats, 65, *65*
  Protein Cookies, 72, 73
  Salmon Crudo with Lemon Chia, 240, *241*
  Spirulina Green Chia Drink, 96, *96*
  Strawberry-Hibiscus Chia Drink, 97, *97*
  Watermelon Chia Refresher, 93, *93*
chicken, 8
  Almond Ricotta and Olive Stuffed Chicken,
    200, *201*
  Chicken and Mushroom Empanadas, 192,
    193
  Chicken Caesar Salad, 146, *147*
  Chicken Chorizo Soup, 120, *121*
  Chicken Fajitas, 194, *195*
  Chicken Tikka Masala, 202, *203*

Coconut-Cilantro Chicken Soup, 118, *119*
  Fried Chicken with Coleslaw and Avocado,
    198, *199*
  Ginger Ale Chicken, 196, *197*
  Peppery Green Salad with Pulled Chicken
    and Lime Dressing, 154, *155*
chickpea flour, 9
chickpeas, canned
  Chickpea Curry Sauce, 318, *319*
  Chickpea Veggie Burgers, 160, *161*
  Curry in a Hurry Burgers, *161*, 167
  Moroccan-Style Baked Fish with Chickpeas
    and Mustard Greens, 182, *183*
chili
  Southwest Chili Burgers, 163, *169*
  Veggie Chili, 116, *117*
  Chimichurri Avocado Toast, Corn and, 294,
    294
  Chipotle Black Bean Dip, 256, *256*
chives
  Ginger-Soy Dipping Sauce, 322, *322*
  Heirloom Tomato Salad, 134, *135*
  Stuffed Bell Peppers, 304, *304*
chocolate, 11
  Almond Butter–Oatmeal Chocolate Cookies,
    340, *341*
  Chocolate-Almond-Coconut Balls, 352, *353*
  Chocolate-Blueberry Cookies, 336, *337*
  Chocolate-Macadamia Smoothie, 77, *77*
  Chocolate-Mint Protein Smoothie, 89, *89*
  Chocolate Protein Truffles, 354, *355*
  Chocolate-Raspberry Smoothie, 86, *86*
  Chocolate Sauce, 330, *331*
  Cocoa-Nutty Trail Mix, 274, *275*
  Cocoa-Raspberry Oatmeal, 64, *64*
chocolate chips, stevia-sweetened
  Almond Popcorn Trail Mix, 266, *266*
  Chocolate Chip Cookies, 344, *345*
  Chocolate Chip Oatmeal Cookies, 340, *341*
  Chunky Monkey Trail Mix, 269, *269*
  Cocoa-Nutty Trail Mix, 274, *275*
  Coconut-Almond Bark, 366, *367*
  Coconut-Espresso Bark, 360, *361*
  Earl Grey Hemp Heart Bark, 358, *359*
  Mulberry-Walnut Bark, 364, *365*
  No-Bake Chocolate Chip Cookies, 338, *339*
  Spicy Pistachio-Goji Bark, 362, *363*
  Trail of Life Mix, 268, *268*
Chopped Salad with Avocado Crema Dressing,
    124, *124*

ABOUT THE AUTHOR

ROCCO DISPIRITO is a James Beard Award–winning celebrity chef and the author of thirteen highly acclaimed books and five *New York Times* bestsellers, including *The Negative Calorie Diet*. Rocco has starred on numerous television shows and is frequently featured as a food and weight-loss expert in print and online media. The healthy lifestyle crusader is the founder of the Pound a Day Diet fresh food delivery service where he personally cooks for and coaches hundreds of clients to wellness. He launched an all-natural product line, Rocco's Healthy + Delicious, featuring an assortment of organic, sugar-free, gluten-free, and dairy-free snacks and meals, available at www .PoundADayDiet.com. He lives in New York City.

Connect with Rocco DiSpirito:

Website: www.RoccoDiSpirito.com
Store: www.PoundADayDiet.com
Instagram: @RoccoDiSpirito
Twitter: @RoccoDiSpirito
Facebook: www.facebook.com/RoccoDiSpirito